POSITIVE RELATIVISM

HARPER'S SERIES ON TEACHING
Under the Editorship of Ernest E. Bayles

POSITIVE RELATIVISM

An Emergent Educational Philosophy

MORRIS L. BIGGE
Fresno State College

HARPER & ROW, PUBLISHERS
New York • Evanston • London

Positive Relativism: An Emergent Educational Philosophy

Library of Congress catalog card number: 78–125322

CONTENTS

EDITOR'S FOREWORD

The purpose, presumably, of stocking the mind is to secure retrieval of any one of the stored items when it is wanted. And, like a well-ordered library, retrieval is readily possible only when a well-ordered and easily understood filing system is in effect. Any worker who understands the system can then, at any time, go straight to a desired item, even though its location or even its existence was previously unknown to him. Logical deduction, not memory, serves as the locational principle.

Thought patterns represent the filing systems of the mind. To be able to "follow the run" of a thought pattern is to understand it. Broad principles or generalizations—high-level abstractions—constitute thought patterns that have high retrieval value; they represent the kind of knowledge that makes transfer readily possible and enables a possessor to find it useful. The only genuinely practical subject-matter content a teacher can teach is basic, tested theory. And to think of philosophy as something other than broad, basic theory is probably to lose for philosophy any legitimate claim to a significant place in education.

Of extant philosophical systems, which furnishes the best organizational base for educational practice? This question is vital for an educational philosopher, and it seemingly should be of first importance for an educational practitioner. Chesterton, when asked whether it is important for a landlady to know a prospective tenant's philosophy of life, countered with the question, "Is anything else important?" This book is one in a series designed to furnish authentic presentations of major contemporary philosophies as they relate to, or impinge upon, educational practice. Each book takes a given philosophy and follows it into its impact or impacts upon such practice. Each author is presumed to be sympathetic to the view he presents and able to speak authoritatively for it. What each philosophy has to offer for education should therefore be discernible in the book devoted to it. Although the general editor and the publisher have not tried to tell any author how he should write his book, they are hopeful that this end will be served.

In addition, publication of the series in the form of separate paperbacks offers flexibility and economy in classroom use: An instructor is thus able thereby to select the specific views he wants studied, whether one or several, and require student purchases of those. Each book in the set is written with the expectation that the others will also be available—hence with no obligation to present any view but its own, even with the necessity perhaps, because of space limitation, to deal with that alone. We hope that the books in this series will prove highly useable and useful.

Ernest E. Bayles

PREFACE

This book is designed for use as a text in introductory upper-division or graduate courses in educational philosophy. It should serve best as the first textbook for a course, to be followed by books that present alternative systematic, normative philosophies. Although it is intended for use in conjunction with introductory courses, it should also provide a high degree of challenge for students in advanced courses in educational philosophy.

Positive relativism is an extension and refinement of the educational implications of the seminal ideas developed by John Dewey.

Although the title is the author's creation and the philosophy is his commitment, many contemporary students of Dewey embrace educational philosophies very much like the one herein developed. Since, to the author, the Progressive Education Movement, as it took form, represented somewhat of a distortion of Dewey's ideas, positivism relativism is in no way a version of Progressive Education. Instead, it is a contemporary representation of a "pragmatic" tradition which has extended from William James and John Dewey through thinkers such as Boyd H. Bode, Arthur E. Murphy, Ernest E. Bayles, and George R. Geiger. However, the tenets of *positive relativism* do not always accord with those of the philosophy of any one of these able leaders.

Some years ago, while the author was pursuing a doctor's degree at the University of Kansas under the excellent guidance of Ernest E. Bayles, he came upon the following statement in Norbert Wiener's *Cybernetics*, "For many years Dr. Rosenblueth and I have shared the conviction that the most fruitful areas for the growth of the sciences were those which had been neglected as a no-man's-land between the various established fields."[1] This struck the author as a vital insight. Consequently, from that time up to the present, he has found his small niche of scholarship in the development of the interrelationships of educational philosophy and educational psychology. Through his professional years he has continued to be convinced that a viable educational psychology should be anchored to a systematic educational philosophy, and that an adequate educational philosophy should be supported by a defensible educational psychology. So this book is a development of a systematic, normative educational philosophy—positive relativism—supported by a coordinate, apposite educational psychology—cognitive-field psychology.

Dewey's ideas were usually expressed in an abstruse style. Yet they can be quite readily grasped when readers realize that his basic writing technique was to develop first one idea—a thesis—then an opposing idea—an antithesis—and lastly a new idea—an emergent synthesis—that transcended both but was not a compromise between them. In broad general terms, his thesis was scientific realism, his antithesis was absolute idealism, and his synthesis was his own pragmatic position. A specific example may be found in Dewey's *Experience and Education*.[2] Here the thesis

[1]Norbert Wiener, *Cybernetics* (New York: John Wiley & Sons, Inc., 1948), p. 8.

[2]John Dewey, *Experience and Education* (New York: The Macmillan Company, 1938).

is traditional education, the antithesis is Progressive Education, and the emergent synthesis is interactive experiential education.

Following the Deweyan tradition, this book first concisely presents the leading traditional philosophic positions on the problem or issue that is being discussed, then it develops in some detail the positive-relativistic emergent synthesis. The author recognizes that because of the limited space available he may deal inadequately with certain aspects of the philosophies—viz., logical empiricism, idealism, existentialism, and rational realism—which represent theses, antitheses, and compromises between them as a first step in development of emergent syntheses. However, he presents the tenets of the respective philosophies as accurately as he knows how, in the hope that even such sketchy presentations will enable students to attain a better grasp of the meaning and significance of positive relativism. Historically, rational realism dates back to ancient Greek civilization. However, ideologically, readers may think of logical empiricism as representing a thesis, idealism and existentialism as representing an antithesis, and contemporary rational realism as representing in some sense a bridge between them. Since the adherents of the verbal-analysis approach to educational philosophy disclaim for it the position of a normative philosophy, there seemed to be little need to introduce this position for the purposes of this book.

Each chapter of the book has been tested in classroom use with both beginning and advanced students. Students have produced extensive oral and written critiques, thereby contributing greatly to the readability and the accuracy of the materials. The author is indebted to many of them for their cogent criticism.

Several persons have helped on the manuscript in various specific ways, for which the author is very grateful. Mrs. Ada Bigge typed various drafts of chapters and has helped to make them more meaningful. Our daughter, Dr. June Lee Bigge, has carefully read the typed manuscript and offered very insightful criticisms and suggestions. Ahmed Hafeez has presented very valuable critiques of the first six chapters. Dr. Laurence Boylan made several excellent proposals for the improvement of Chapter Six. Dr. Frederick C. Neff has reviewed the total manuscript and made many excellent suggestions for the improvement of both its substance and its final form. With all its shortcomings, the book is much better than it would have been without the competent assistance of these fine friends.

M.L.B.

1

How is Positive Relativism an Emergent Educational Philosophy?

A systematic philosophy is a generalized blueprint for the projection of people's attitudes toward attempts at a more adequate and harmonious way of thinking, living, and acting. An educational philosophy is a systematic philosophy centered upon the proper role of schools in development of their goals and the means for achieving them. Accordingly, an educational philosophy is a general theory of education; it is centered upon, but not restricted to, a study of man.

A teacher, to the utmost of his ability, needs to think through his principles, values, and purposes with all of his intellect, feeling, and imaginative capacity. When he is immersed in this process, he is being philosophical, and the results of his cogitations are aspects of his educational philosophy.

In embracing an educational philosophy, an educator has at least three possible choices. He may conform rigidly to one systematic philosophy; he may eclectically—selectively—borrow from the various outlooks and arrange his ideas into a mosaic or patchwork, which is available for him to draw upon as need arises; or he may develop an *emergent synthesis*—a somewhat new, systematic outlook which benefits from knowledge of previously developed philosophies but is not an eclectic compromise between them. Although eclecticism has its strengths, its basic weakness is that one dedicated to it has no defensible, systematic basis for knowing when to use discrete aspects of respective positions. Thus, the choice of outlook and method for each situation is largely a matter of whim or chance.

An *emergent* is something novel which appears in the course of evolution of ideas. It is not an intermediate position, but a genuinely new outlook or concept. When an emergent outlook reflects the results of the interplay of conflicting ideas and arrives at something new, it is a *synthesis*. Whereas one forms an eclectic compromise by selecting aspects of opposing theories and taking a position somewhere between them, one achieves an emergent synthesis by selecting and modifying knowledge from incompatible positions, adding new thinking as needed, and developing a new position which is internally consistent and still more adequate than its precursors.

Positive relativism functions as an "emergent synthesis" capable of transcending many of the difficulties underlying other positions and at the same time providing a philosophical basis for a set of school practices that reflect a knowledge of pertinent scientific evidence and that are both adequate and internally consistent. Adherents of positive relativism take into account the philosophical contributions of logical empiricists, idealists, rational realists, and various compromises between them. However, they develop an emergent synthesis from these various lines of thought rather than form an eclectic compromise that, if achieved, would very likely take the form of a hodgepodge.

To help readers grasp the ideological bases for the emergent ideas of positive relativism, we intersperse throughout the book some very brief statements in regard to the tenets of idealism and rational realism and some much longer statements concerning the logical-empiricist position. Both logical empiricism and positive relativism are empirical philosophies. Their being empirical means that they emphasize that man's learning centers in perceptual experience as contrasted with *speculative* reasoning. However, these two educational philosophies differ sharply in their definition of experience (see pp. 46–48) and therefore in their interpretations of the nature of learning. So, one may enhance his understanding of positive relativism by seeing just how its various aspects differ from those of the tougher-minded logical empiricism.

Logical empiricists are convinced that the physical world experienced by human beings is real and essentially what it appears to be when observed through the senses. Furthermore, even if there were no human beings around to observe it, it would exist in the same state. Therefore reality, like existence, is independent of a thing's being known. Logical empiricists assume that the physical world is governed by natural laws, which operate inexorably and without change. They further assume that a basic principle of the universe is sequential cause and effect; every event is determined by events that have gone before. Thus, the universe is a vast mechanism governed by laws, which are essentially mechanical in nature.

A logical empiricist is likely to think that there is a kind of hierarchy of the sciences, some being much more objective and reliable than others. He places at the top of the hierarchy physics and chemistry, aided by mathematics. These sciences are regarded as models which other sciences should emulate. To a consistent logical empiricist, nothing should be asserted to be real or meaningful unless, through observation, it can be subject to objective study, using only publicly verifiable data. If anything exists, it supposedly exists in some amount; if it exists in some amount, it can be measured. So, logical empiricists think that we should abandon "dogmatic, other-worldly, supernaturalistic, tender-minded, rationalistic, parochial preconceptions and . . . replace them by critical, worldly, naturalistic, fact-minded, empirical, experimental, and universally applicable ways of thinking."[1]

Logical empiricists assume the existence of an ultimate reality,

[1] Herbert Feigl, "Aims of Education for Our Age of Science: Reflections of a Logical Empiricist," in *Modern Philosophies and Education*, Nelson B. Henry, ed. (Chicago: The University of Chicago Press, 1955), p. 306.

which consists in fixed natural laws, and they define truth as that which corresponds to natural law and, consequently, is unchanging. Contrastedly, *positive relativists* neither assert nor deny an absolute existence. Rather, they define psychological reality as that which we "make" of what we gain from our environment. They then deal with a reality so defined in achieving truth and designing behavior. Thus, whereas for a logical empiricist reality is the same as an objective existence, for a positive relativist reality is psychological and thereby different from any objective existence; it is what people gain through use of their five-plus senses.

In contrast with *logical* empiricism, positive relativism is a *psychological* empiricism; its efforts are centered upon the logic of growing minds or intellects, functionally defined. Hence positive relativists neither assert nor deny the reality of an absolute existence which is either physical, mental, or both. Instead, they center their intellectual activity on a different focus—experiential situations.

For an *idealist,* a substantive mind or consciousness is at once the very stuff of the universe and the root of the structural forms of this stuff. Human consciousness in its seemingly intimate and personal aspects is a more or less errant variant of the universal mind. The basic tenets of an idealist are that his origin is within the mind of the deity, his basic nature is a substantive mind with a free will with which the deity has endowed him, and his purpose on earth and eventual destiny are immortality.

Rational realists build their thinking around the concept of a human biological organism, as viewed by logical empiricists, accompanied by the idea of a substantive mind, as conceived by idealists. Rational realists are convinced that all human life has a "form," which, if we can apprehend it, will give us an insight into the standards appropriate for the "good life"—an absolutistic concept.

Positive relativism is a *unique contemporary version* of an indigenous American educational philosophy which was formerly identified as the pragmatic outlook. Pragmatism was introduced and developed by Charles Sanders Peirce, William James, and John Dewey. Since the basic tenet of pragmatic philosophy is that ideas and actions should be evaluated on the basis of their humanistic fruits rather than any metaphysical roots, the outlook has spearheaded a sweeping redefinition of man and the nature of his knowledge and his learning process.

During the past seventy or eighty years, positive relativism has been emerging as a constructive reaction against the absolutistic ways that have characterized many facets of men's thinking throughout recorded history. Within any absolutistic system of thinking, facts are asserted to be eternally true; they are supposedly the direct result of either observation or intuition, and truth is taken to be ultimate and final. Positive relativists reject absolutistic ways of approaching the study of man and human learning. Consequently, positive relativism contrasts with the various absolutisms as a basic frame of reference within which man and his learning process may be studied. Because of its historical underpinnings, many aspects of this current educational philosophy are either explicit or implicit in the voluminous writings of John Dewey.

Positive relativism, like other systematic educational philosophies, is a basic outlook which colors the thoughts, ideals, and actions of its adherents. However, rather than its being a device for dealing with problems of philosophers as such, it is a method and outlook, spearheaded by philosophers, for dealing with the problems of men. Accordingly, positive relativists characterize a systematic philosophy as neither a speculative pursuit nor a method of detached analysis, but as a systematic outlook that may provide a foundation for a program of living. They then construe educational philosophy as a study of such an outlook as it is related to teaching and learning. Now, let us examine the respective meanings of *relativism* and *positive* as they are combined to delineate an educational philosophy.

A central idea of *relativism* is that any object derives its qualities not merely from something inside itself but from the total situation, i.e., its surroundings as well as itself. In other words, no object has meaning apart from its context, and a thing, event, or idea derives its qualities or meaning from its perceived relationships with other things, events, or ideas. A person may look at a patch of grass which is in a shadow. Compared with grass in the full rays of the sun, the patch appears dark; but compared with grass at night, it appears light. A homely girl in the company of girls even more homely appears pretty. Thus, the way we perceive any object or event is colored by the total perceptual situation, and we deal with objects relationally rather than as things in themselves. This principle is actually one with which everyone is familiar. Relativistic philosophy does little more than explore and develop the numerous ramifications and implications of this central idea.

It might appear that, if relativism were a valid concept, a person could never make a definitive statement about anything, except to say that it is "closer" than something else, it is "to the left" of something else, it is "darker" than something else, or it is "smaller" than something else. However, this is not an insurmountable problem. In order to view a thing relativistically, one simply determines a convenient vantage point for reference.

A man can say that his automobile has 200 horsepower, and in such an assertion he can be quite confident. The unit of measure, one horsepower, is an arbitrary standard contrived by man and susceptible to future change, yet it has definite usefulness as a point of reference. Such relatively fixed points of reference are *relatively absolute*. The word absolute, so used, is an adjective; it means no more than that the point of reference is one of relative fixity or stability. The noun *absolute*, in contrast, connotes a supposed existence outside any context, an existence in itself as such.

The term *positive* differentiates this kind of relativism from nihilism, which may also be called "relativism." Nihilism— "nothing-ism"—means that life is meaningless and useless. Since nihilists make their relativism absolute, they hold a pessimistic outlook which denies the possibility of any genuine basis for truth and moral principles. Positive relativists, in contrast to the nihilists' pessimism, are melioristic. Meliorism, a positive relativistic tenet, is an emergent synthesis arising from the contrast of the absolutistic positions, pessimism and optimism. Meliorism implies that there is little basis for the assumption that matters are inevitably getting either better and better or worse and worse. It further signifies that, since conditions can be improved through growth or learning, we should constantly try to make them better. (The Latin word *melior* means "better.")

It is important to note that positive relativists do not deny the existence or even the subsistence—abstract, eternal existence—of absolutes. Instead, they define reality and truth relativistically and assert no position in regard to absolute existences. However, they do think that the question of what something may be when totally independent of any observer or frame of reference is scientifically meaningless. The functional application of a concept, not its metaphysical roots, is a positive relativist's criterion of its truth and value.

The "positive" aspect of positive relativism denotes that such a relativism, to quote Webster, is "logically affirmative" and "capable of being constructively applied," as in "positive proposals for the betterment of society."[2] Accordingly, to say that positive relativism is affirmative means that its proponents assert the availability of truth and reality and thereby affirm the feasibility of a body of constructive knowledge. Furthermore, its capability of being constructively applied signifies that it is structured in such a way as to direct its adherents toward promotion of further development, improvement, and advancement of themselves and society.

A person is being positive-relativistic in his thinking when, being uninfluenced by his commitment to any absolutes, through the use of his human intelligence he endeavors either to improve conditions or develop something better to take their place. Hence, the goals and ends of an individual's thought and behavior are to be found within the possibilities of present situations projected into the future; they are in no sense final and absolute. Furthermore, all valid ideas or propositions are construed as instruments of human progress—individual, collective, or both—that may be achieved through processes of reflective thinking.

The basic orientation of positive relativists centers on the following points:

1. Formation of an emergent synthesis derived from a study of logical empiricistic objective principles and idealistic subjective tendencies.
2. Subordination of interest in any absolutistic concepts to concern with purposive human endeavors.
3. Opposition to the idea that knowledge is a spectatorial report in regard to a given, fixed reality waiting to be uncovered.
4. Interpretation of experience as a process of interactive cooperation between a knower and the known within which manipulation, conceptualization, and control replace merely looking on and reporting.
5. A joining of theories of knowledge and theories of values.
6. Acceptance of an open-endedness of knowledge—no ceiling is placed upon man's potential.
7. Emphasis upon a democratic outlook both in and outside schools.

The ideology of positive relativism embraces at least six major facets, each of which is treated in turn in subsequent chapters. Each facet is introduced as a chapter title in the form of a sig-

[2] *Webster's Third New International Dictionary*, s.v. "positive," definition 4a (1).

nificant question. Following the introductory chapter, (1) the principal contents of subsequent chapters are (2) the purposively interactive psychological nature of man and his motivation, (3) relativistic suppositions concerning the nature of reality and man's perception of it, (4) the nature of relativistic truth and value, (5) a positive-relativistic treatment of learning, (6) a school's place in a democratic society, (7) the implications of positive relativism for classroom practice, and (8) the nature of reflective teaching and learning processes.

2

How is the Psychological Nature of Man and His Motivation Purposively Interactive?

Since positive relativists think that a person does the best he knows how for whatever he conceives himself to be, their primary concern is with the psychological nature of man. Other aspects of positive relativism are developed in relation to its basic position in regard to the nature of human nature. So, man's image of himself is of crucial significance. To quote Rollo May: "The critical battles between approaches to psychology . . . in our culture in the next decades, I propose, will be on the battleground of the image of man—that is to say, on the conceptions of man which underlie the empirical research."[1]

The mammal *man* has certain distinguishing characteristics which give him a unique quality as an object of study. First of all, he is capable of speech and he is a time-binding animal—both past and future enter into his present perception of things. He is moreover an animal with a culture: he builds on his past in a peculiarly selective fashion. Then, he has a unique capacity for social interaction with his fellows which enables him to transcend concrete situations and live in a more or less imaginative sphere. Most significant of all, however, is the fact that in his perceptual process he is capable of viewing himself simultaneously as both the subject and the object, as a knower and a known.

Although some educational philosophers give only a minor place in their philosophy for a basic psychological outlook, each philosophy, to a large degree, actually rests upon its adherents' particular conception of the basic nature of human beings. Man's most significant nature, then, is a psychological one. One way to approach a study of his generic psychological nature is to consider the character of his basic, innate moral and actional nature; what general psychological features characterize all members of the human race?

Basically, we may assume man's generic *moral* nature to be either *good, bad,* or *neutral*—neither—and his *actional* nature to be either *active, passive,* or *interactive.* If we assume that man is naturally evil, then we can expect nothing good from him. His evilness will naturally unfold if left to itself; he will show no traits other than bad ones. Contrariwise, if we assume that man is naturally good, then, unless he is corrupted by some outside force, everything that comes from him will be good. Neutrality in basic moral nature means that we assume that man by nature is neither good nor bad, but merely *potential* in a way that has no connection with innate badness or goodness.

If people are basically *active,* their underlying characteristics are inborn—thus, psychological reality comes from within them. Environments merely serve as locations for their natural unfoldment. If they are basically *passive* or *reactive,* their characteristics are largely a product of environmental influences. Hence reality is centered in environment. If persons are *interactive,* their psy-

[1] Rollo May, *Psychology and the Human Dilemma* (New York: Van Nostrand Reinhold Company, 1967), p. 90.

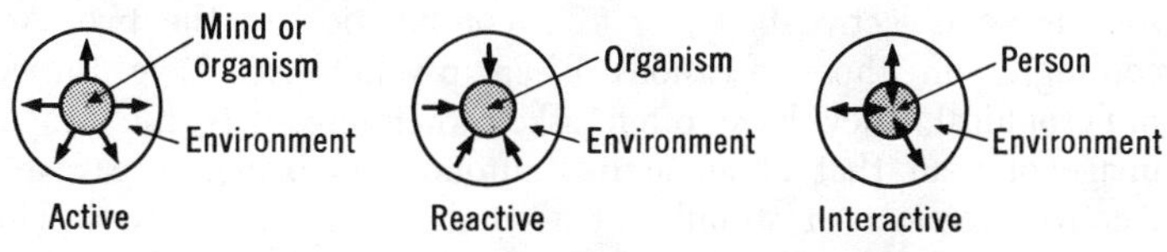

FIGURE 1. Models of mutually opposed assumptions in regard to the basic nature of men and their environmental relationships.

chological characteristics result from their "sizing up" their physical and social environments as they relate to them; thus reality is person-environment centered; it consists of what one makes of what comes to one—that is, what one gains from experience. These three mutually opposed assumptions in regard to human beings and their environmental relationships are illustrated by the three models in Figure 1.

When we consider the ways in which it is possible to combine assumptions concerning man's basic moral nature with those concerning his relationship with his environment, we might reasonably assume that students, by nature, are either good-active, bad-active, neutral-active, neutral-passive, or neutral-interactive.

The *good-active* assumption points toward either philosophical idealism or romantic naturalism. If we should assume students to be either *bad-active* or *neutral-active,* we would embrace the rational realist tradition in philosophy and, in educating them, we would adhere to some form of mental discipline—mind training. *Neutral-passivity* is the presupposition of logical empiricists; it leads to some sort of behavioristic stimulus-response conditioning theory in dealing with students. So, throughout this book behaviorism and conditioning theory are used interchangeably to denote the psychological position of logical empiricists. (The terms *behaviorism* and *conditioning theory* as herein employed embrace all behavioristic psychologies. These include Watsonian behaviorism, Thorndikean connectionism, conditioning not accompanied by reinforcement as developed by Guthrie, and the neobehaviorisms as represented by Skinnerian operant conditioning or reinforcement.) Lastly, the assumption that man (including all students) is *neutral-interactive* is the pivotal concept of positive relativism and cognitive-field psychology.

In their attempt to study man with the prevailing methods and techniques, psychologists have tended to oversimplify him. Thus, they have usually viewed man either as a subjective mind or person, as an objective body, or as a combination of the two. Accordingly, on those occasions when psychologists have turned philosophical, they have often asked themselves: Is the proper image of man that of an active, autonomous being? a passively reactive recipient of stimuli? or a combination of the two? The concept of man as an active autonomous being is rooted in *idealism;* the idea of him as a passive recipient of stimuli is rooted in *logical empiricism;* and the idea of his being both harmonizes with the *rational realist* philosophical approach. In contrast to all three of these views, the supposition that man's nature is neutral-interactive, the basic tenet of cognitive-field psychology, complements *positive relativism.*

Present-day emphasis upon the subjective nature of man is rooted in Roussellian natural unfoldment and various instinct and basic-needs theories as exemplified by Freudian psychology. Current subjectivism takes the form of a psychedelic humanism within which a person, completely on his own, is sufficient for every situation. He arrives at decisions on all issues in accordance with the way he feels, and he is completely confident that he is right. Leaders in promulgating this subjective emphasis promote each individual's intuitive awareness of himself and the artistic expression of his self-actualization. One's feelings are taken to be the final authority for truth. Consequently, there should be no coercion, no prescription, or no imposition of any values or truths.

Positive relativists think that, since a person is a psycho-social being, there is no such thing as a person in total isolation. Thus, an era of wholly self-determined men probably never did and never will exist. Personal development is largely a matter of individual-social development. To quote Sigmund Koch, "This entire, far-flung 'human potential' movement [of psychedelic humanism] is a threat to human dignity. It challenges any conception of the person that would make life worth living, in a degree far in excess of behaviorism. Yet its message is surprisingly akin to that of behaviorism."[2]

Logical empiricism, as contrasted with idealism, treats man within a behavioristic frame of reference as basically an extremely well-designed, clever machine who learns through accumulating memories in an additive process. Human responses are a chance affair without intentional purpose, and a human being is a biological organism with a history of conditioned behavior. Accord-

[2] Sigmund Koch, "Psychology Cannot Be a Coherent Science," *Psychology Today*, September 1969, p. 68.

ingly, for a logical empiricist, words such as foresight, purpose, and desire are literary terms, but not scientific ones.

Logical empiricists and their behavioristic psychological counterparts continue to think in terms of stimuli being causes and responses being effects and of there being a time lapse between physical stimuli and organic responses. To quote Hebb, "Temporarily integrated behavior, extended over a period of time, is treated as a series of reactions to a series of stimulation. . . . Stimulus followed directly by response is the archetype of behavior. . . ."[3]

Positive relativists challenge logical-empiricistic statements which imply that propositions of psychology must likewise be physicalistic ones. Thus, they do not agree with Hempel, who thought that "psychology is an integral part of physics."[4] They consequently contend that, since men cannot adequately explain themselves as persons in terms of physics, chemistry, and biology, they need a psychology that is a science in its own right. Although they do not assume that significant human behavior is determined by *prior* causes, they do think it can be scientifically predicted. Accordingly, they seek contemporaneous causal relationships, not a sequential, cause-effect order of human behavior. To be scientific, one need not necessarily be physicalistic or reductionistic. Although a denial of mechanistic causation from a physical point of view may well be foolhardy, an educational philosopher or psychologist as such should not be primarily concerned with any mechanistic, physical causation of human behavior.

Some thinkers see the dual subjective and objective nature of man as constituting a genuine dilemma or paradox. Rollo May has stated: "*The human dilemma is that which arises out of man's capacity to experience himself as both subject and object at the same time.*"[5] In a similar vein, Carl Rogers has said:

> It is my conviction that a part of modern living is to face the paradox that, viewed from one perspective, man is a complex machine. . . . on the other hand, in another dimension of his existence, man is subjectively free; his personal choice and responsibility account for his own life; he is in fact the architect of himself. . . . If in response to this you say,

[3] Donald O. Hebb, A *Textbook of Psychology* (Philadelphia: W. B. Saunders Company, 1958), p. 46.

[4] Carl G. Hempel, "The Logical Analysis of Psychology," in *Readings in Philosophical Analysis*, Herbert Feigl and Wilfred Sellars, eds. (New York: Appleton-Century-Crofts, 1949), p. 378.

[5] *Op. cit.*, p. 8.

"But these views cannot both be true," my answer is, "This is a deep paradox with which which we must *learn to live*."[6]

But positive relativists surmount this dilemma through development of the idea that man is not half passive and half active, but *interactive*.

In the process of development of an emergent synthesis from the two horns of the active-passive or subjective-objective dilemma, cognitive-field educational psychology has emerged as a significant aspect of positive relativism. Learning is not to be equated with unfoldment and sheer expression of inner urges. Nor is it a conditioning process which comes from the environment's impinging upon a biological organism from without. Rather, cognitive-field psychologists find the clue to the meaning of learning in the aspects of a situation within which a person and his psychological environment come together in a psychological field—life space.

The basic concept of cognitive-field psychology, then, is *life space*, which is explained in some detail on pages 17–19. The life-space metaphor provides a pattern for thinking, as contrasted with a picture of any absolute existence. It cuts below the splitting of man between body and mind and deals with him in terms of his distinguishing characteristics as man.

The purpose of cognitive-field psychology is to formulate tested relationships that are predictive of the behavior of individual persons in their specific life spaces. In order to understand and predict such behavior, one must consider a person and his psychological environment as a pattern of interdependent facts and functions. Cognitive-field psychology is an interpersonal, social psychology, which constitutes an effective vehicle for characterization of man. It integrates biological and social factors and treats respective persons as interacting with them. In the interactive process a person and his psychological environment are construed as interdependent variables. Thus, a person is neither dependent upon, nor independent of, his environment. Likewise, a person's environment is neither made by him nor independent of him. Thus, whereas behavioristic psychologists are biological-organism centered, cognitive-field psychologists are psychological-person centered. "Organism'" suggests a mechanism and human passivity; "person," in contrast, suggests purposiveness and interactivity.

Cognitive-field psychologists establish order, but they go about it in a different way than do behaviorists. Along with benefiting

[6] Carl Rogers, "Freedom and Commitment," paper delivered at San Francisco State College, 1963.

from the experimentation done under other banners, they develop their own unique type of scientific research. Experimentation within cognitive-field psychology involves the study of such matters as cognitive processes, the recall of uncompleted tasks, the relationship of levels of achievement and levels of aspiration, psychological ecology, group dynamics, action research, concepts of self, personality rigidity, individual and social perception, and reflective teaching.

HOW IS PURPOSIVE CHOICE AN EMERGENT SYNTHESIS?

Whereas traditional rational realism and idealism generally hold that man is endowed with a *free will*, logical empiricism adheres to *determinism*, which is the opposite of the concept of free will. Contrasted with both, positive relativism emphasizes *situational choice*—at any juncture of his continuous, overlapping life spaces, a person may to some extent choose which way he is going to turn next. Within idealism or rational realism, a man's free will is his sovereign faculty, distinct from, and superior to, his sensory desires, physical impulses, and emotional cravings; it has its source beyond his world of experience. Thus, a mental, substantive will is the force which guides, molds and directs the life of man. The will is endowed with the power to choose between motives and to act or refrain from action. Commitment to the idea of free will involves the conviction that at a choice point one *went* one way but *could have* gone the other. Therefore, in the event that one has made the wrong turn, one should be conscious of guilt.

Determinism denies the existence of a will that is free, holding instead that all man's acts result from some combination of reflexes, instincts, stimuli, sensations, feelings, associations, and habits which forms their antecedent cause. Whereas adherents of the freewill position make much of personal guilt for past actions, determinists assert that whatever the person did in a given situation is the only thing he could have done. For the determinist there is no logical basis for guilt. The freewiller, on the other hand, is convinced that even though he did act in such and such a way in a given situation, he could have willed, and consequently done, otherwise.

Positive relativists, and likewise cognitive-field theorists, postulate that men exercise choice, but they neither assert nor imply identification with either side of the metaphysical freewill-determinism antinomy. They simply mean, to quote Dewey, that "every intelligent act involves selection of certain things as means to other things as their consequences."[7] At a choice point or in a situation, a person does decide which way to go. But his exercise of choice does not imply the operation of a free will even though the choice is not the product of prior determining factors. Rather, human intelligent action is taken to be immanently purposive, and it is best interpreted only when it is seen in the light of the goals it is designed to achieve. So, being immanently purposive means that goals arise within one's world of experience. Immanent, purposive choice is an emergent synthesis arising from the antinomy of transcendental free will and mechanistic determinism. (Immanent means remaining within the situation at hand.)

Within cognitive-field psychology, "purposive" is virtually a synonym for "intelligent." A unique characteristic of human beings is their capacity to pursue longsighted, as well as shortsighted, self-interests. When a child or youth is behaving purposively, he is pursuing his goals in light of the insights he has available; he is behaving intelligently. The goal or goals toward which the individual strives psychologically exist in his present life space. The phenomenon of goal is such that expectation—not actual realization—is its essence. Although the content of a goal may be in the future or may not occur at all, the goal as a psychological fact necessarily lies in the present life space. For example, a student's goal to become a teacher is a goal toward teaching as he now sees it. This goal may be a far cry from teaching as it is eventually experienced.

To repeat, the purposiveness of cognitive-field psychology is immanent in (operating within) not transcendental to (extending beyond) the world of experience; it prevails in workaday life situations. That is, careful study of children and youth, as well as of other animate beings, in life situations indicates that if they are active at all, they are trying to do something, and that it is only through anticipating what they are trying to do that we can predict most accurately what they are going to do. Purposiveness, so construed, merely means that an individual acts in such a way as to achieve his goal or goals—satisfy his wants or desires—in the quickest and easiest way that he comprehends or senses as possible under existing conditions. When one is motivated toward

[7] John Dewey, *Logic: The Theory of Inquiry* (New York: Holt, Rinehart and Winston, Inc., 1938), p. 460.

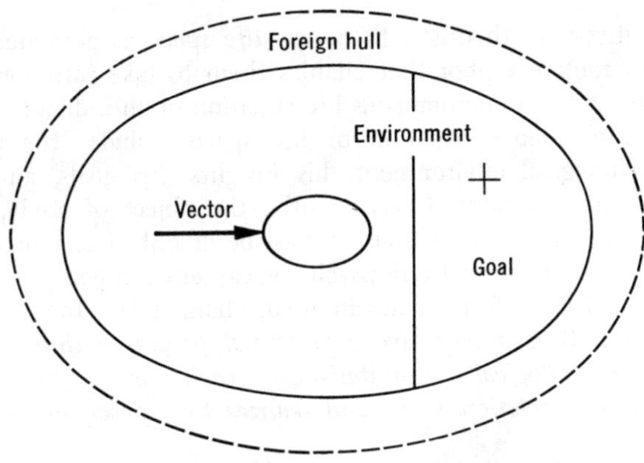

FIGURE 2. A life space and its foreign hull.

doing something, his description of the matter is that he wants or desires to do it. So, one's conscious activity is carried forward to a goal by a process of constantly searching out the conditions for the next step all along the way. Since positive relativists use cognitive-field psychology as their medium for a psychological study of man, their understanding of the concept *life space* is highly essential.

WHAT IS A LIFE SPACE?

The life-space concept is a scientific formulation of a series of nonrecurring but overlapping situations, each replete with its unique propensities and relationships. It is developed for the purpose of (1) expressing what is possible and impossible in the life of a person and (2) anticipating what is likely to occur. It is therefore uniquely a psychological phenomenon. A life space represents the total pattern of factors or influences which affect an individual's behavior at a certain moment or a longer juncture of time (see Figure 2). Behavior is any change in a life space which is psychological—in accordance with a growing intelligence. As a child develops, he lives through a more or less continuous and overlapping series of life spaces. Each life space of a moment or longer juncture contains a person and his psychological environment of that moment or juncture; it is characterized by the interaction of the two.

Cognitive-field theorists, then, use *life space* as a model, paradigm, or root metaphor that enables them to take into consideration the total contemporaneous life situation of an individual. Such a contemporaneous situation or life space includes the person, his psychological environment, his insights, his goals, and their dynamic interrelations. Consequently, the object of study, when applied to man, is a unit that can best be described as a-discerning-person-in-interaction-with-his-psychological environment; this is a life space. *Interaction*, as herein used, characterizes the nature of perception. It *is a cognitive experiential process within which a person, psychologically, simultaneously reaches out to his environment, acts in relation to it, and realizes the consequences of his action.*

All psychological events—acting, thinking, learning, hoping, dreaming—are functions, not of isolated properties of an individual or his environment, but of mutual relations of a totality of coexisting facts that constitute a life space. A life space represents, not physical objects as such, but functional and symbolic relationships. Hence, it includes not only presently perceived objects but also memories, language, myths, art, anticipation, and religion. A series of an individual's life spaces are not discrete but overlapping, and a continuous series of overlapping life spaces represents the total psychological world in which a person lives. This psychological world may include the person's precepts, knowledge, and beliefs; his forward and backward time perspective; and abstract ideas as well as concrete objects.

A life space consists of functional regions, each having a positive or negative valence. It is surrounded by a foreign hull—the aspects of the physical and social environment which to that person at that juncture are not psychological. The foreign hull of a life space consists of all the potential perceptions as contrasted with the actual functional perceptions of a person's unique field.

A person, his psychological environment, and the foreign hull of his life space are represented by concentric figures. A person is within his psychological environment and both are within the foreign hull. Nonpsychological factors observed only by an outsider can at the next moment become psychological for the person being studied. There can be movement both ways through the boundary of a person or a life space or through any of their regions. For an aspect of the physical world to influence the intelligent behavior of a person, it must be moved from a foreign hull into his life space through his interaction with it.

It is important to keep in mind that the essence of a life space is its functional nature; it represents not physical entities but functional relationships. It therefore constitutes an instrument whereby one may be objective in studying human behavior by being, to some degree, subjective. A teacher may conjecture, "What would I be thinking if I were a student and were acting that way?" or "If I were in his situation, why would I be acting the way he is?"

It should also be remembered that a diagram of a life space is figurative. It is difficult, perhaps impossible, to show everything at once. A complete and accurate image of a life space would show all of the psychological facts and constructs in a total situation represented by a differentiated person and a differentiated environment. A differentiated person or environment is one structured—functionally divided—into various aspects as perceived by the one being studied. Some differentiated aspects of a person are friends, ambitions, self-aggrandizement, and needs and abilities to know about various matters and to carry out activities of different kinds. A differentiated environment contains everything perceived by the person at the time under study.

Also, we should guard against reifying or making physical things of the psychological constructs whose purpose is to symbolize relationships primarily functional in nature. For example, we should at no time think of a psychological person as synonymous with a biological organism, or of a psychological and physical environment as the same concept.

Should the reader at this time desire a more expanded treatment of the life-space concept, he is referred to Chapter 5, pages 77–81. Especially he should see Figure 3, page 78, and Figure 4, page 80.

For an adequate understanding of the concept *life space,* one needs to grasp the idea of *contemporaneity* and to see how *person* and *psychological environment* interrelate in a series of contemporaneous situations.

WHAT IS THE PRINCIPLE OF CONTEMPORANEITY?

Contemporaneity means literally "all at one time." A psychological field or life space is a construct of such nature that it contains everything psychological that is taking place in relation to a specific person at a given time. The unit of time viewed microscopically is a moment; however, considered macroscopically it may cover hours or even weeks. Whatever the length of time, everything is going on at once—that is the meaning of "field." Some forty years ago, George H. Mead wrote, "We live always in a present whose past and whose future are the extension of the field within which its undertakings may be carried out."[8] More recently, an eminent social psychologist, Gordon W. Allport, has stated:

> My own position, which goes under the designation *functional autonomy of motives,* holds that motivation may be—and in healthy people usually is—autonomy of its [historical] origins. Its function is to animate and steer a life toward goals that are in keeping with *present* structure, *present* aspirations and *present* conditions.[9]

Kurt Lewin, the founder of field psychology, also emphasized that behavior depends on neither the future nor the past but on the present field. To quote him, "Since neither the [physical] past nor the [physical] future exists at the present moment it can not have [immediate] effects at the present."[10] Use of the concept *psychological field* implies that everything which affects behavior at a given time should be represented in the field existing at that time, and that only those facts which are part of a present field can affect behavior.

The principle of contemporaneity means that psychological events are determined by conditions at the time behavior occurs. One cannot derive behavior from either the future or the past as such. Both behaviorists and cognitive-field psychologists see little basis for supposing a future cause of present events. However, cognitive-field psychologists differ sharply from behaviorists in their insistence that any attempts at derivation of behavior from the past is equally metaphysical—beyond the realm of science. Since past events do not now exist, they cannot as such have any effect on the present. Thus, influence of a future can only be anticipatory, and effects of a past can only be indirect. Nevertheless, through the continuity of life spaces, past psychological fields do have their "trace"—residue—in a present field which

[8] George H. Mead, *The Philosophy of the Present* (LaSalle, Ill.: Open Court Publishing Co., 1932), p. 90.

[9] Gordon W. Allport, *Personality and Social Encounter* (Boston: Beacon Press, 1960), p. 29.

[10] Kurt Lewin, *Principles of Topological Psychology* (New York: McGraw-Hill Book Company, 1936), p. 35.

influences a person's behavior. *Trace* is a region or condition of a present life space that has similarity to a characteristic of earlier life spaces. In other words, "trace" means that there is some similarity between regions of succeeding life spaces. When, in solving a current problem, a person uses an insight acquired earlier, the insight is an example of trace.

In order to understand a person's present personality structure, it is often convenient and perhaps necessary to inquire into the individual's personal history. But such inquiry is merely a means of knowing the present structure of his life space. A person's psychological field that exists at a given time contains, as well as the environment of the present, the views of that individual about his future and his past. It should be emphasized that any psychological past or psychological future is a simultaneous part of a psychological field existing at a given time. Psychologically, there is no past nor future except as it enters into the present.

An individual's views about the past, as about the rest of the physical and social world, are often incorrect; nevertheless, they constitute a significant psychological past in his own life space. Furthermore, the goals of an individual as a psychological fact lie in the present, and they too constitute an essential part of his life space. The contents of the goals may lie in the future, and they may never occur; but the nature of an expectation is not dependent upon the event's coming to pass. If an Indian warrior were brave in order that in the future he would go to the happy hunting ground, whether or not a future happy hunting ground actually existed would have no bearing on his being brave. His happy hunting ground is a part—a goal region—of his contemporaneous life space.

WHAT IS A PSYCHOLOGICAL PERSON OR SELF?

Cognitive-field psychologists place one's *person* at the center of his psychological field. A person is that body or configuration of matters with which an individual becomes identified, of which he takes care, and to which he gives his allegiance. So defined, it is not a fixed quantity or static thing. It is *achieved*, as contrasted with being inherently possessed.

Under no circumstances is a person considered identical with an organism. Thus, a person is not limited to a mind or body;

neither is it a mind and body. Rather, a person is *a consciously behaving self*. It is the center of abilities and needs, and it is what a child means when he says "I" or "me." The concept *person* may be considered synonymous with *self*. Whereas teachers more often think of Billy Smith and Sally Anderson as persons, Billy and Sally, when thinking of themselves, are more likely to use the term "self."

A person is in no sense an abstract ego which can be experienced apart from any social context. It is within the social living of an individual that a person emerges and continues to change throughout life. It may be said that the basic human need is for preservation and enhancement of this emergent self or person. One even owns a "loyal" dog in order to enhance and give constancy to one's psychological person.

How does a child construct his self?
A young child, to a greater extent than an adult, is a dynamic unity. When he cries, he cries all over; when he is hungry, all of him is hungry; and when he is frightened, he is startled completely. Consequently, he perceives his self only as he distinguishes it from his environment and various aspects of it from one another. The rather sharp distinction between one's person and one's psychological environment is something which grows in an individual's thinking, as the "I" or "self" is gradually formed. However, one's person grows so that soon the central feature of his social and personal motivation becomes the maintenance and furtherance of the welfare of that self.

A child's awareness of his self is manifested in at least four different ways: (1) he reaches certain results by his own efforts and comes to feel responsible for his acts, priding himself on his achievements and blaming himself for his failures; (2) his self, being embodied in values and goals, is realized in his transactions with other people; (3) as he evaluates his conduct over against an ideal, an ideal self emerges (people often identify this ideal self with "conscience"); and (4) his self grows to a prominent place in his memories of a past and his anticipations of a future.

Under normal conditions an individual's self is likely to involve his strongest motives. When a child uses the term *I, me, mine, you, yours, he* or *she, him* or *her*, or *his* or *hers*, a self is emerging. Such concepts arise only as a person interacts with other individuals and groups of people. Through this interactive process each person acquires such achievements as language, conceptual

thinking, and n
sights.

Are selves always
So far as we kno
tween his body a
his life space is c
a child lives and g
an attempt to hav
about him as he se
vironment. In turn,
his life space leads
vironment. It is in t
facts acquire their ps
it has encased itself i
Moreover, any self in
inconsistent selves or
In its widest possibl
tion of all that he cal
body, his speech, his th
his grandparents, his br
groups, his personal pr
concerns and the instit
justs to his social and p
self with the activities or
person and *interests* a
phenomenon. The conte
cherished ideals and intere
of interest actively taken i
one's selfhood or personh
or concerned is a brief wa
actively his person and his

How many selves does an in
In a sense, a person has a
distinct groups for whose o
Jimmy Jones at home is one
another, and on a football fiel
maintains a variety of interes
and so might be said to have
However, although there is a c
space of an individual, we can

such nature that
pushes the othe
each person, if
made up of his
there is some de
chological struct
period of time,

HOW

A person's psy
physical and s
engaged at a
because it is
environment is
is immersed.
optical, acous
and his psyc
dependent bu
To repeat,
person and h
is always sur
son's life spa
which, at th
psychologica
hull has ph
and social c
spaces. Any
ment, but
hull of his
any way,
foreign hul
Althoug
usually m
them. As
each with
the one t
a new lif
different
tinuity o

As succeeeding nonpsychological physical and social environments—foreign hulls—are outside their respective psychological environments, they can have no immediate effect upon a person's intelligent behavior. However, through interaction with the environment, parts of a present foreign hull are transformed into goals, barriers, and other psychological factors of future life spaces. They are then no longer a part of the foreign hull. Factors so transformed become parts of subsequent psychological persons or environments. Thus, what a moment before constituted only part of the foreign hull may at the succeeding moment be a central part of the person or his psychological environment.

Since each person's perceptual environment is unique, it is obvious that two persons may appear to be in the same location in space and time (or as nearly so as possible) and yet have very different psychological environments. Furthermore, the behaviors of two equally intelligent persons who are confronted with the same "objective facts" may differ radically because each is different in his purposes and experiential background. Whenever a person has a new experience, he changes his environment; he will never be able to recapture the old environment in its identical form. The cognitive-field conception of environment helps explain why in a particular family one son may become a minister and another turn to crime; their interpretations of their world differ radically, even though to an outsider their social and physical environments would appear quite similar.

Although physical and social environment furnish a setting—matrix—for the psychological environments of individuals in a group, they are quite different from the psychological environment of any one member of the group. Hence, we should never identify a child's physical or social environment as it appears to others with his psychological environment.

HOW IS MAN'S MOTIVATION PURPOSIVELY INTERACTIVE?

Within cognitive-field psychology, a person's motivation develops through his differentiating his life space into regions and subregions—functional objects and activities—and simultaneously through his cognitively structuring the regions and subregions by grasping some of their meaningful relationships. As new regions and subregions emerge, they also are to some degree structured cognitively; that is, they are made meaningful in line with the person's purposes.

Motivation, then, is goal-oriented. The concept of man as interactive implies his having a dynamic quality. Motivation occurs, not because of past experience or conditioning, but as an aspect of a current psychological situation. It arises when one perceives an inadequacy, disharmony, or inconsistency in one's values, outlooks, attitudes, or actions.

A person's living in a world entails his living in a series of situations. *In* as it is used here has a distinctly different meaning from *in* when used in regard to beans in a can or money in a purse. It is more like the meaning of a bee in a swarm. A person is *in* a situation and the situation is *in* the person. Thus, perceptual interaction is taking place between the two—the person and what at that time constitutes his psychological environment.

A human life, then, may be considered to consist of a series of distinguishable person-environment interactions within which neither objective physical nor objective social factors have a one-to-one psychological relation to a child. There is probably no known way that a child can experience the absolute nature of things-in-themselves. What he does experience is *that which he makes* of what he gains from his environment as he pursues his various goals. Consequently, it is in connection with personal goals that situation-centered needs enter the scene.

What are the nature and the source of needs?

A positive relativist is convinced that problems concerning the origin of motives cannot be adequately solved by studying only the physiological or physical origins of needs. Furthermore, needs cannot be ascertained and identified through mere observation of facial expressions, "startle" reactions, visceral changes, and electrochemical responses. Nor can they be found simply by observing gross behavior of children.

A *need* is a state of a person that, when it exists in relation to a goal, induces behavior toward that goal. The state of a person in itself does not cause behavior; part of the environment—a perplexity or a goal—must also be operative before a psychological situation can exist. When a person is perplexed, he feels a necessity to do something but has no good idea of what to do; he has a need even though he has not yet formulated a definite goal in relation to it. In a psychological situation needs and goals, although not identical, are closely interrelated. Accordingly, a person's behavior may be described either as his trying to reach his goals or as his trying to satisfy his needs. However, goals and needs are in no sense mutually exclusive. Goal achievement and need satisfaction are accomplished through the same process of intelligent action.

A need is equal to a psychological tension which is manifested in goal-seeking behavior. To quote Lewin, "A need corresponds to a tension system of the inner-personal region of a life space."[11] The inner-personal region of a life space consists of matters which are most vital to the person. His cognitive (knowing) and manipulative (doing) abilities are functionally located between his needs and his environment. These abilities are used in the development of understandings of, and relationships to, the person's environment.

Psychological needs do not arise within an organism or from an environment, but only through one's interaction with his environment. Hence, it is only through perception and manipulation of the environment that a person delineates tasks for himself—he develops tensions and needs.

Behavior in a specific situation usually stems from a combination of several needs, a "derived need." Furthermore, during his lifetime a person's needs constantly change in intensity and degree of differentiation. Nevertheless, many of his needs and other features of his successive life spaces remain approximately the same over long periods of time. This latter tendency is called a "continuity of life spaces." There are, however, periods of crisis in a person's development when quick and striking changes in needs occur, even in those needs for which a high level of continuity had been established.

How are valences related to needs?

Cognitive-field psychologists identify the imperative or challenging facts of an environment as its *valences*. For a particular child, psychological facts may include dogs, cats, rooms, chairs, knives, friends, things that fall down, things that turn over, things that start and go, things that take one places, things that go up and down, places where one is safe from danger, and places where food is available. These things and places lead a child to play, sit, eat, ride, climb, hide, and manipulate. It is in connection with these psychological functions that valences or attractions of en-

[11] *Ibid.*, p. 218.

vironmental objects and activities derive their strengths. Valences are the aspects of an environment which make it attractive or repulsive; thus they are either positive or negative.

It is a person's interaction with his environment that gives a thing valence. The valence of an object or activity usually arises from the object's being a means of, or barrier in the way of, satisfying a need. Thus, the valence of environmental objects and the needs of a child are correlative, and the valences of factors of his environment determine the direction of his psychological development or movement. The particular objects or activities which bear valences, and the strengths of their valences, are quite different for a baby, a kindergartner, an adolescent, and an adult. A child's insistence on independence in some activity indicates that that activity has taken on a definite valence and that a part of the child's goals has become the enhancement of his "self." A child of three trying to jump down a step may refuse help. The step, to him, has a definite valence. Unless he reaches certain results by his own effort, he will not be content. This is evidence of emergence of a self—of his psychological development.

By means of experimentation readers may observe how, through a person's ego- or self-involvement, valences of his activities arise along with corresponding personal needs. The experiment may involve any activity of such nature that the subject can set goals of differing degrees. The activity might be high-jumping, distance swimming, or making a chain of paper clips. Ask the subject what he thinks he will achieve, and place his goal at that level. Permit the subject to compete with himself and provide his own motivation; thus, do not say, "How far do you think you can go?" The subject's goal is the cross-bar placed at a certain level on the standards, the spot to which he hopes to swim, or the number of clips he will assemble in five seconds. As the subject makes tries and sets new goals, a relationship will develop between what he achieves in one trial—his *level of achievement*—and where he sets his next goal—his *level of aspiration*. He will set his goal at a point that he thinks he might achieve but is not certain he will. If he falls far short, he will lower his goal. If he reaches his goal, he will raise it the next time.

If left to decide for himself, a person will set his goal at a point which he thinks he probably, but not surely, can reach. Since there is a possibility of failure, attainment of the goal will give him a sense of success; for success to be success there must be a possibility of failure. When left to choose between several goals, a person will prefer the goal which is more difficult to reach, provided he anticipates a possibility of reaching it and it is not identical with other goals easier to reach. Everything else being equal, a child will prefer a toy which is slightly more difficult to reach; but if he is permitted to choose between tools with which to get the toy, he will prefer the tool which is in easier reach. The law of parsimony—least action—holds for psychological means but not for psychological ends. A professor walks to the campus to give himself exercise, but when he *heads* for the campus he cuts every corner along the way.

A valence, then, is an "imperative environmental fact." It is a property of a region—functional part—of one's environment that draws the person psychologically toward it or impels him away from it. Thus, as contrasted with needs, which are person-oriented, valences are focused in environment. When a boy has a strong need for a bicycle, the valence of a bicycle is high. So *valence* and *value* are similar concepts. A child's person-centered needs and abilities parallel his environment-centered goals and valences. But to speak of needs as centered in person and of goals and valences as centered in environment does not mean that they are *located* in these respective places; they are located in a situation or life space—in both person and environment. Centeredness merely means a closer identity with one than with the other.

Although needs and valences contrast in being focused respectively in person and environment, they are also very closely related. The valence of a certain object or activity depends partly upon its nature and partly upon the state of the relevant needs of the person at the time. Consequently, any statement regarding change of needs can be expressed by a statement about positive and negative valences. For example, an increase in the intensity of a need (for instance, the need for recreation) leads to an increase in the positive valence of certain activities (going to the movies or reading a book) and an increase in the negative valence of certain other activities (doing hard work).

Positive relativists regard the traditional separations of organism from environment, individual from society, and a personality from its culture as false, or at least misleading in their consequences. Although they place great emphasis upon individuality, they also recognize the fact that individual needs are closely related to social influences. The culture in which a child grows affects, though it does not determine, practically every one of his needs. The needs of a growing child are changed, and new needs induced, through the influence of social groups with which he identifies himself. His needs are also influenced by the ideologies of groups to which he would like to belong and of those from which he desires to be set apart.

Thus, throughout a situational approach to needs, it is recognized that without a culture or society a human being would probably be devoid of personality and of psychological needs. The matrix of each personality and its needs consists of the customs, beliefs, attitudes, values, and habits of the group within which a child grows. However, the form which needs take depends upon how individuals interact with the institutionalized behaviors of a culture.

WHAT IS BEHAVIOR?

In cognitive-field psychology and positive relativism, the term *behavior,* when used, is interpreted quite differently from the way that both behaviorists and logical empiricists commonly define it. The latter, in harmony with their interpretation of psychology as a study of the relationships of biological organisms and their physical and social environments, think of behavior as some kind and degree of measurable, and publicly observable, muscular or glandular movement. The movement may be only incipient or covert or it may be overt; nevertheless, its being behavior means that it is physical movement. Were adequate devices available, it could supposedly be observed and measured. Positive relativists do not accept this definition of behavior. For them, psychological behavior involves purpose and intelligence; hence it is not correlated one-to-one with physical movement. Furthermore, it is not directly observable but must be inferred.

In speaking of behavior, positive relativists imply psychological locomotion but not necessarily any sort of physiological movement. One may "come closer" to another person, yet exhibit no physical evidence of locomotion. Behavior takes place in a life space, rather than in observable space. Psychological behavior is more or less conscious—verbal or symbolic—and may be equated with experience. Every specific instance of behavior must be viewed as the result of the interaction of several pertinent features of a concrete situation. Then, broadly defined, behavior means any change in a life space which is subject to psychological laws. Behavior may therefore be a change of the relative location of a person and his environment, a cognitive reorganization of his environment, or a restructuring of his person. It also includes any change in valence of any part of his life space.

Psychological behavior and *locomotion* are analogous concepts. *Behavior* describes the simultaneous functional changes within a life space of an individual. *Locomotion* refers to the relative positions of respective regions of a person's *temporally continuous* life spaces. When we concentrate study upon a person and his current environmental situation, *behavior* adequately denotes changes that occur in a life space. However, when we consider a time element, a person appears to occupy a series of overlapping life spaces. The life spaces usually manifest a continuity; they are similar but not identical. Change in subsequent life spaces is locomotion. Consequently, depending upon whether we are centering our study upon the person-environment interactivity or the psychological continuity of a person's life spaces, we may interpret any psychological change in terms of either behavior or locomotion; behavior centers upon how one sizes things up, locomotion on what one does about it as he moves into a new life space. So, psychological behavior may be (1) an overt purposive act, (2) an attitudinal shift, (3) a change in the perceived value of an object or activity, or (4) a new relationship established between two or more events.

3

WHAT IS REALITY AND HOW IS IT PERCEIVED?

The philosophical problem regarding the nature of reality is called *ontology*. Thus, ontology is "is-ology": What is the nature of the being of Being? In its historical sense, the term *reality* has been an absolutistic one. The presumption back of its use has been that there is a preexistent metaphysical reality, which transcends any and all perceptions of it. Within an absolutistic frame of reference, the ontological pursuit has been, not to question the meaningfulness of the concept *reality*, but to determine the nature of existence as an aspect of metaphysical reality.

For contemporary logical empiricists the term *reality* likewise connotes a transcendental, independent, and absolute existence. Logical empiricists have accordingly tended to treat reality and existence as identical concepts. For them, *reality* refers to physical objects and processes which exist, or are "out there," in their own right. The chair on which the reader is sitting may be said to exist, and to a logical empiricist the chair is a good example of *reality* (not one's impression of the chair, but the chair itself). The chair exists in its own right; the way one perceives it is not relevant to its reality. A. J. Ayer, a leading logical empiricist, equates existence with *reality*, and he asks, "Can there be any doubt at all of the present existence of the table at which I am seated, the pen with which I am writing, the hand which is holding the pen? Surely I know for certain that these physical objects exist?"[1]

In contrast with logical empiricists, positive relativists consider any philosophical commitment to dealing with a known permanent world of reality of things, with their own objective characteristics existing in and of themselves apart from one's perceptions, to be an imaginative fallacy. Yet they recognize that, unless a person lives in a *supposed* world with some degree of constancy, he cannot effectively fulfill any purposive activity. (A supposed world is one believed to *be*, or accepted as such.) But they think that "the reality of things in our objective worlds is their significance to us in carrying out our individual purposes,"[2] and that it is "meaningless to inquire into the absolute correctness of a conceptual scheme as a mirror of reality."[3]

So, it is futile to attempt to define a transcendental reality which, if it does exist, is not now and may never be known. Accordingly, "our classical, inherited view of nature as an object 'out there' is an illusion, . . . the subject is always part of the formula, . . . the man viewing nature must be figured in, the experimenter into his experiments or the artist into the scene he

[1] A. J. Ayer, *The Problem of Knowledge* (Baltimore, Md.: Penguin Books, 1956), p. 125.

[2] *The Morning Notes of Adelbert Ames Jr.*, Hadley Cantril, ed. (New Brunswick, N.J.: Rutgers University Press, 1960), p. 162.

[3] William Van Orman Quine, *From a Logical Point of View* (Cambridge, Mass.: Harvard University Press, 1953), p. 79.

paints."[4] Although positive relativists do not deny the independent existential nature of physical data, they do emphasize that the only reality with which one can deal is what one *makes of* what physical nature seems to be.

Whereas variations of logical empiricism, idealism, and rational realism that have emerged earlier than positive relativism have made ontology the central problem in philosophy, positive relativism reduces ontology to a marginal operation. Actual problematic experiences crowd the hazy background of things in themselves, independent existences, immutable essences, ultimate ideas, and fixed absolutes from the center of attention. (A problematic experience is one within which a person is faced with a conflict—no-road or forked-road—situation and desires to find his way through it.)

To repeat, positive relativists do not deny the independent existence of objects, but they make no attempt to define a transcendental reality of objects or ideas which, in case they do exist, can not be known as such. Instead, they build their thinking around that which can be scientifically verified. Arnold Brecht has written:

> Indeed, the old philosophical question of reality, insofar as it aims at the ultimate Truth behind all possible astronomical, physical, chemical, and biological discoveries is beyond the province of Scientific Method by definition, since it is metaphysical in character and Scientific Method does not answer metaphysical questions.[5]

Positive relativists describe reality, but not existence, in psychological or perceptual terms, not in "objective," physicalistic ones. Accordingly, they replace logical empiricists' substantive doctrine of the independent existence of reality with their positive relativistic functional concept of *perceptual interaction.* Thus, relativistically—i.e., experimentally and situationally—defined, perceptual interaction is the process of persons making sense of what they gain through their five-plus senses, and reality consists of what they make of that which they gain through their five-plus senses and their manner of "sizing it up." The meaning of reality within the framework of perceptual interaction is therefore the key to understanding positive relativism and how its ideology

[4] Rollo May, *Psychology and the Human Dilemma* (New York: Van Nostrand Reinhold Company, 1967), p. 10.

[5] Arnold Brecht, *Political Theory* (Princeton, N.J.: Princeton University Press, 1959), p. 53.

contrasts with that of logical empiricism—a kindred but critically different empirical approach.

Positive relativists, then, make a distinction between reality and existence. Without denying the independent existence of objects, or even of other people's ideas, they insist that each person sizes up or interprets his world in such a way as to form a meaningful pattern for himself, and his interpretation of his world is the reality on which he designs his actions. Thus, they think that a person's knowledge of things is always limited by the impossibility of his ever getting completely "outside himself." However, whereas they do not assert the existence of a real external world independent of all perceptions of it, they do recognize that a generalized concept of a physical-social world provides an experiential ground for individuals' perceptions of their respective experienced worlds. Accordingly, whereas positive relativists recognize that any person acts as if he thinks there is some sort of physical-social world within which he lives, they also assume that any perception of a physical-social world will be colored to some degree by the purposes and experiences of the observer and by the procedures used in observing the object perceived. None of these statements, however, should be taken to mean that a person literally makes his world. Rather, in any field—science, social relations, morality, even religion—each individual makes, *not the world,* but *his notion of the world.*

So positive relativists operate in relation to a supposed "common sense" world of commonality which provides raw material for individuals' perceptions. But a perceptual world is always an individual one. A supposed world of commonality is one accepted as such on much less than conclusive evidence, or in other words it is one thought probable. In summary, whereas the common world is a supposed one, one's perceptual world is a presumptive or prognostic one. Whereas a supposed world provides nonpsychological foreign hulls for life spaces, perceptual worlds are life spaces, insights into which provide guides for intelligent actions.

WHY METAPHYSICAL NEUTRALITY?

"Metaphysics" means literally *after* physics, but *beyond* physics gives us a more accurate sense of its current meaning. Metaphysics includes ontology, the problem of being; cosmology, the problem of the nature of the order of being; and teleology, the problem of the universe's being endowed with purpose. The term *metaphysical* means of, or relating to, what is conceived to be supersensible, and consequently transcendental to man's sensory experience. Thus, metaphysical reality is an ultimate reality, one which lies beyond the observable world; it is a reality which underlies its physical manifestations.

In developing a philosophy appropriate and highly pertinent to public schools, positive relativists do not assert either that there is or that there is not a supernatural or transcendental metaphysical existence. They simply note that persons size up their perceived worlds as they find them in a way which makes things fall into a pattern, and that a perceived world is something significantly different from one accepted as a matter of absolutistic commitment. Consequently, they emphasize that in a pluralistic nation committed to religious freedom and separation of church and state, our public schools (and also our nonparochial private ones) should be made truly secular institutions. Accordingly, they neither ridicule nor reject supernaturalism and transcendental teleology; they merely set them aside as not pertinent to the educational job at hand. Whenever they are serving in their unique teaching capacity, public school teachers should promote critical intellectual activity, not metaphysical formulations. Accordingly, they should restrict themselves to secular functions.

"Secular" is derived from the Latin word *saeculum*, which means "finite time." Thus, secular matters are those belonging to the present, empirical world as contrasted with nonsecular matters, which relate to an eternal, metaphysical world. Whereas what people have done or are doing about religion is a secular matter, people's religions as such are nonsecular. The historical fact that certain peoples have believed in the immortality of souls is a secular concept. But the immortality of souls is a nonsecular one. A school's restricting its studies to secular matters means that it should not raise those scientifically unanswerable metaphysical questions about which man has been, is now, and will continue to be concerned. But it should study the nature of such questions and the history of their introduction into the thinking of mankind.

Since in our democratic society, both within and outside school, each individual citizen must have complete freedom to hold any metaphysical, nonsecular position he chooses, a teacher should not appear either to favor or disfavor *any* student's metaphysical or nonsecular beliefs. Public schools should confine their operations to secular matters, and public school teachers as such should assume a neutral stance in relation to all nonsecular commitments regarding the nature and destiny of man. Thus, teachers as such should neither assert nor deny the intervention of supernatural or teleological forces in the affairs of men. In this way, schools would adhere to the dictum, as stated by Justice Frankfurter, that "no religion shall either receive the state's support or incur its hostility."[6]

In the past, pragmatic educational philosophers and teachers (forerunners of positive relativism), in their very teaching procedures, have often violated a basic tenet of their own pragmatic philosophy: their antagonistic stance in relation to metaphysical questions, as opposed to the neutrality which might better characterize their attitude, has frustrated their students instead of perplexing them or challenging their ingenuity. Instead of seeking to involve students with real problems, thereby bringing them to make frontal attacks on such problems, pragmatists have often attacked students' metaphysical beliefs to the point at which the students have become deeply frustrated and, psychically, have either withdrawn from the scene or become militantly aggressive —two evidences of frustration. Psychologically, they have resorted to flight or fight. The consequence has often been that under pragmatic tutelage only the few students who truly underwent existential experiences have gained very much from their philosophical study.

Positive relativists, then, are neutral in regard to any reality except that which can be dealt with through critical intellectual activity in the form of problem solving, scientific method, and reflective thinking. Thus, they emphasize critical intellectual activity as opposed to speculative, metaphysical formulation. In this way they take the principle of relativity seriously into account.

Many positive relativists think that the historical outlook in which men have pictured a fixed, absolute reality—a reality affirmed to exist independent of any perception of it—has been a great stumbling block to progress in the modern world. Boyd H. Bode has expressed this succinctly: "The creation of this transcendental world was at the same time one of the most brilliant achievements and one of the major tragedies of human civilization."[7] However, it should be iterated and reiterated that a posi-

[6] See Sam Ducker, *The Public Schools and Religion* (New York: Harper & Row, Publishers, 1966), p. 78.

[7] Boyd H. Bode, *Progressive Education at the Crossroads* (New York: Newson & Company, 1938), p. 22.

tive-relativistic educational philosopher as such does not assert either that there is or that there is not a supernatural, nonsecular existence. Since his system of thinking does not depend for its validity upon nonsecular existences, it simply does not assume, and is not based upon, the actuality of any form of supernatural being.

The need for public schools to confine their educational activities to secular matters in no way implies that teachers should exclude the study of moral values from their classrooms. Instead, they should promote the historical study of various possible ideological foundations of morality, and simultaneously emphasize that in all classroom deliberations a secular basis for morality should be sought. Since secularly developed values have an empirical basis, they should be given an importance equal to that of any other subject matter. However, it should be left to students' home or other extraschool relationships to develop any metaphysical sanctions for the value systems which may be fostered at school.

Since positive relativism has emerged as a constructive, positive reaction against the absolutistic ways that have characterized many facets of men's thinking throughout recorded history, it is neither negativistic nor absolutistic in any manner or degree. Its being non-negativistic means that it is neither atheistic, agnostic, nor skeptical. Atheism is an absolutistic doctrine that there is no deity. Agnosticism is commitment to the belief that the form of existence of God or Ultimate Reality is unknowable. However, unlike atheism, it does not assert that there is no God. Skepticism centers upon uncertainty or doubt; so, it too is negativistic in its approach to knowledge. The positive characteristic of positive relativism sets it off from any negativistic approach to the meaning of reality.

Positive relativists carefully avoid the use of any and all forms of absolutes. The term *absolute* is derived from the Latin word *absolvere,* which means to set free. Accordingly, the noun *absolute* refers to "1*a*: something that is independent of human perception, valuation, and cognition"[8] or that which is not dependent upon anything beyond itself. "More recently the term [absolute] has been extended to mean . . . the All or totality of the real, however understood, and . . . the World Ground, whether conceived idealistically or materialistically, whether pantheistically,

[8] *Webster's Third New International Dictionary,* s.v. "absolute."

theistically, or dualistically."[9] Thus, when a thing or idea is absolute, it is both unlimited and independent of its context. Accordingly, when one asserts the absolute nature of a thing or concept, one declares that it is free from conditional or mental limitations.

Some philosophically absolute realities that may be supposed to exist are mind, truth, intelligence, beauty, goodness, and morality. However, any or all of these concepts may also be construed relativistically, and positive relativists are convinced that men can use the concepts much more profitably when they are so conceived. Therefore, relativistically defined, actuality may take various forms which may also be called mind, truth, intelligence, beauty, goodness, and morality. In later chapters, each of these is treated within a positive-relativistic frame of reference.

Positive relativism is based upon the premise that ultimate metaphysical reality as a thing-in-itself, if such exists, is unknowable through perceptual means, though not necessarily unbelievable to man. Consequently, positive relativists see little point in concerning themselves with attempts at the observation of ultimate existences as things-in-themselves. Nevertheless their purpose is not to destroy men's ability and desire to speculate about the nature of absolutes, but rather to promote their recognition of the limits within which the results of such cogitations are applicable. They thus leave the way open for students to believe what they will about absolute existences, so long as their beliefs do not impede their devoting their full intellectual energy to the acquisition and use of scientific, reflective knowledge—knowledge tested by its functional consequences.

WHAT IS PERCEPTUAL INTERACTION?

Within the cognitive-field psychology of positive relativism the meaning of a sensation or perception is always related to the total situation. So, relationships, not a summation of individual elements, determine the quality of any event. Furthermore, any psychological event is the result of the interaction of many factors; hence, perception always involves a problem of organization. Also, whatever is perceived is modified within the more or less concrete

[9] Dagobert D. Runes, ed., *The Dictionary of Philosophy* (New York: Philosophical Library, Inc., 1942), p. 2.

perspective of the perceiver. Then, a thing is perceived as a relationship within a field that includes the thing, the viewer, and a complex background incorporating the viewer's purposes and ongoing experience. In view of these notions, it is obvious that to a positive relativist the senses do not directly mirror physical objects in their geographical environment. Moreover, perception is highly selective: it is always related to a person's purposes at the time of perception. In his goal-seeking behavior, a person actively identifies those aspects of his environment that will help or hinder him, and usually it is to these that he is primarily sensitive.

To repeat, perceptual interaction is a cognitive process within which a person, psychologically, simultaneously reaches out to his environment, makes something of it, acts in relation to it, and realizes the consequences of his action. Within the process, a dynamically purposive person, who is at the center of a contemporary configuration of both himself and his environment, derives his qualities or characteristics through an operation which is something other than either an active or a reactive relationship with his psychological environment. In contrast with these types of relationships, perceptual interaction is a process of a person's "making something of" what he gains from his environment, his being interactive.

The basic principle of interaction is that nothing is perceivable or conceivable as a thing-in-itself; no object has meaning apart from its context. Hence, everything is construed in relation to other objects. More specifically, a thing is perceived as a figure against a background, experienced from a given angle or direction of envisionment. Persons in a given culture have a common social matrix, and a person devoid of a society is a rather meaningless concept. Still, each person is unique in both purposes and experiential background, and the reality upon which he bases intelligent action consists of himself and what he *makes of* the objects and events that surround him. Thus, in perception, a man and his perceived environment are coordinate; both are responsible for what is real.

Relativistically speaking, the "reality"—psychological environment—with which a person interacts consists of what he makes of the things he gains through his senses or any other sources available to him. Consequently, the meaning of any object arises from one's interpretation of the relationship between the object and oneself. When one interacts with an object or activity, he sizes it up. When a child sees a tiger as a kitty, psychologically it is a kitty; and a kitty which adults call a tiger is a part of the child's psychological environment.

See if you can get the point of this story concerning what makes a ball a ball and a strike a strike. What is the significance of the statement of the third umpire (a positive relativist)? How does his statement differ philosophically from the statements of the first two umpires? And what positions are represented by the statements of the first two umpires?

The story concerns three baseball umpires who were discussing the problems of their profession. The first umpire said, "Some's balls and some's strikes and I calls 'em as they is." The second umpire said, "Some's balls and some's strikes and I calls 'em as I sees 'em." While the third umpire said, [I sees 'em comin' and] "some's balls and some's strikes but they ain't nothin' till I calls 'em."[10]

Positive relativists think that a person is never indifferent toward anything that he is perceiving. A thing is to some degree valent—valuable—or he would not be perceiving it. Furthermore, perception of an object involves not only what one senses and feels about it but also what one is inclined to do in regard to it. Accordingly, this is a *relativistic*, as opposed to an absolutistic, mechanistic, way of viewing man and his perceptual process.

A mechanist attempts to explain the fullness and variety of a universe in terms of machinelike objects and movements. Thus, a mechanist considers a person an organism that is a product of its unique history of stimulus-response patterns. He consequently reduces all human activities to movements, usually in terms of stimuli and responses. Just as an automobile is built by workmen who assemble its respective parts, a person is educated by teachers who feed into his physiological makeup the various aspects of environment which supposedly make him what his teachers want him to be. Of course, his teachers, too, are products of mechanistic conditioning. So they also can do only what they actually do.

A positive relativist makes no attempt to relate psychological behavior to a biological organism and its physical or geographical environment *as such;* in cognitive-field psychology, the psychological concept *person* is much broader than is the biological concept *organism*. So,

through his coping experiences the child discovers and measures himself, and develops his own perception of who and what he is and in

[10] Hadley Cantril, "Perception and Interpersonal Relations," *American Journal of Psychiatry*, August 1957, p. 126.

time may become. We can say that the child creates his identity through his efforts in coming to terms with the environment in his own personal way.[11]

Within positive relativism, perception is interpreted in its broadest possible sense. Thus, it does not mean mere consciousness. There is evidence from observation of human and animal behavior that one cannot use consciousness as the sole criterion of what is part of a life space. A child playing in his yard behaves differently when his mother is home and when she is out, yet he probably at no time verbalizes—is specifically conscious of—her being home or away. Children in a schoolroom with teacher A conduct themselves quite differently from when they are with teacher B. Yet they may at no time consciously formulate the two patterns of behavior. Likewise, dogs and other animals size up situations and do the best they can for themselves; however, there is little if any evidence that in so doing they carry on a conscious process. Perception, then, must be so interpreted as to cover all the different ways one has of getting to know his environment.

In apparently the same kind of instance, a person at different times may perceive quite different aspects of a situation and behave accordingly. Furthermore, the fact that the opportunity is provided for one to perceive certain aspects of a physical or social environment in a certain way by no means guarantees that this particular perception will occur or that the perception that does occur will have anything like a one-to-one relationship to the objective environment as it appears to someone else. Adelbert Ames, E. Engel, and Hadley Cantril have performed experiments at the Institute for Associated Research, Hanover, New Hampshire, which show that in perception nothing is absolutely fixed. Rather, one interprets everything in terms of the situation as a whole. What one perceives—one's reality or life space—consists of what one makes of what seems to be oneself and one's environment. Depending on the habits—insights or understandings—a person brings to a particular occasion, he seems to give meaning and order to things in terms of his own needs, abilities, and purposes.[12]

Perceptual interaction, then, is an encounter within which an

[11] Lois Murphy *et al.*, *The Widening World of Childhood* (New York: Basic Books, Inc., Publishers, 1962), p. 374.

[12] These experiments are summarized in Alfred Kuenzli, *The Phenomenological Problem* (New York: Harper & Row, Publishers, 1959), Chap. 8.

individual structures himself and his environment in terms of the relevance of their various aspects to the achievement of his goals. Within the perceptual process our world is transformed, but not created, by the very operation in which we experience it. Furthermore, our confrontation by our environment is not a photographic-plate process; instead, it is a selecting, excluding, rearranging, modulating, and restructuring one.

In the interactive process, the two key concepts are *person* and *psychological environment*. The paradigm *life space* is used to illustrate, understand, and predict their mutual relationships. A *person* is what one makes of one's organism and all other features which he thinks of, or deals with, as *his*. His environment is what he *makes of* what seems to surround him. A person's life space consists of the content of the individual's perception. His psychological environment, therefore, is not an undifferentiated medium in which he is immersed but is rather what he "makes of" his physical-social environment, and it consists of everything around him which has any meaning for him. Thus, it contains everything that a person purposively can do anything about. So, a psychological environment is distinctly different from a physical one. Whereas the physical environments of a group of students in a classroom are relatively the same, each of their psychological environments is unique. (*Life space* is explained on pages 77–80.)

IS INTERACTION OF PERSON AND ENVIRONMENT ALTERNATING OR SIMULTANEOUS AND MUTUAL?

The term *interaction* is commonly used in describing the person-environment process through which reality is perceived. Both logical empiricists and positive relativists use the term, but they define it in sharply different ways. Whereas logical empiricists mean the *alternating reaction* first of organism, then of environment, positive relativists always imply that the interaction of a person and his environment is *simultaneous* and *mutual:* both participate at the same time, and the two—person and environment—are not mutually exclusive of one another.

Logical empiricism and alternating reaction

Alternating reaction—passive interaction—begins with a reaction of a person to a stimulus. The person is regarded as a passive receiver of stimuli; his habitual pose is one of waiting or repose. When he receives a stimulus he reacts in whatever way he must —in accordance with the habits or the conditioned and innate behaviors that are called into play. When he reacts, it is likely that he will change his physical or social environment in some way. (The environment is also passive in the sense that it "waits" for him to do something to it.)

To a logical empiricist, the temporal sequence of the interactive process is stimulus-reaction-stimulus-reaction, and so on. The chain of S-R's may continue indefinitely. Consider an example. A dog bites a man; the man kicks the dog. Let us suppose the kick conditions the dog not to bite. The dog is friendly toward the next man he encounters, and the man reacts by patting him on the head. The dog may then react by licking the man's hand. The man may then buy the dog a steak. And so on, ad infiinitum.

Logical empiricists think of interaction as involving only physical processes. That is, material objects react to other material objects. Interaction between human beings, therefore, is analogous to the interaction of molecules in a chemical compound. One molecule strikes another, which is deflected against another, which hits another, and so on. Thus, the interactive process is regarded as a chain of causes and effects; stimuli are causes and responses are effects.

Positive relativism and simultaneous mutual interaction

Interaction, when used by positive relativists and likewise cognitive-field psychologists, refers to a relationship between a person and his environment in which the person in purposeful fashion tries to give meaning to his environment and use objects in it in advantageous ways. As he interprets and uses his environment for his own purposes, both the person and his environment are changed. However, the person's physical environment may, or may not, be changed in ways which others may observe. But in any case, its meaning is changed so that it looks different to the person interacting with it. The person also changes in the sense that through his interaction with his environment he achieves new insights which really transform him, in however minor ways. Now, gone from this concept of interaction is the idea of the reaction of a passive organism to a stimulus, and an ensuing chain of S-R's running back and forth from organism to environment. Rather, we now have a simultaneous mutual relation of a person and his environment during which the two are not mutually exclusive, so we do not make a sharp distinction between them. In symbolic terms, this concept is simultaneous mutual interaction—the *SMI concept.*

Parents and siblings usually constitute important aspects of a child's environment. When a second child arrives in a family, the first child sizes up—perceives—the situation. Whether the first child feels rejected depends not upon the physical stimuli as such that he receives from his parents and sibling, but upon what he makes of the relationship of the parents and the second child. The important question is not, Do the parents actually favor child number two? but rather, Does child number one "see" child number two as favored over child number one—himself? In this situation, the parents and the other child are key aspects of each child's and parent's environment. The way child number one perceives the situation has important bearing upon the environmental nature of child number two and the parents.

Cognitive-field theorists and positive relativists, in their espousal of the SMI concept, make a sharp distinction between interaction of physical objects in a physical environment and the subject of psychology—interaction of psychological realities in a psychological environment. A person interacts by relating himself, as he understands himself, to his interpretation of what is around him. Of course, while interacting, he may move his body and manipulate objects in his physical environment in ways obvious to an observer. But to positive relativists, psychological interaction and physical reaction are two different processes. A person can interact within a psychological field while he is seated in an armchair in front of a fireplace. Human experience is synonymous with an interactive event. It does not necessarily require any kind of motion that an observer can detect.

Any idea can be ridden too hard, and the reader probably has already thought of cases in which the concept SMI does not seem to fit. For example, a man who is not aware of danger may be shot in the back. It seems fairly clear that in such a case the man has been a passive victim of a feature of his environment that was active in relation to him. However, all this example suggests is that there are situations in which a person has no control over what happens to him. Cognitive-field psychology and positive-relativistic philosophy do not deny this; instead, they operate on the not inconsistent assumption that whenever a person can, he seeks to manipulate purposefully all those aspects of his environment that mean something to him at the time. He may or may not be successful, but whether or not he is, his life space will be different as a result of the attempt.

A positive relativist's perceptual world contrasts with an idealist's intuited universe of mind, a logical empiricist's observed mosaic of independently existing things and relations within which man is both a spectator and a part cf a running machine, and a rational realist's world of both intuitional minds and experienced things. A positive relativist's world is one of *experience* within which his acquisition of knowledge is a process of testing ideas and thoughts experimentally—scientifically and reflectively—to see what works.

WHAT IS EXPERIENCE?

The concept *perceptual interaction* leads to a unique interpretation of experience. Experience, within positive relativism, is a psychologically insightful event which involves a person's acting partly overtly and partly symbolically and realizing the consequences of the action either overtly or symbolically or both. So defined, experience is a process of perceptual interaction of a person and his psychological environment. Within the interactive process, person implies environment and environment implies person; each concept requires the other. Furthermore, expansion of self is also expansion of environment, and vice versa.

Positive relativists regard experience as a pivotal concept in any discussion of the interactive process and the meaning of reality. Logical empiricists, in contrast, generally avoid using the term, especially in connection with any investigation or description which is supposed to be scientific. Most logical empiricists charge that positive relativists use the term *experience* in such a way as to imply the existence of a process that does not involve the real physical world at all, but only "mentalistic" copies of it. According to logical empiricism, the concept *experience* presupposes a special world of consciousness, and even if consciousness does exist, it does not lend itself to scientific study. So they contend that usage of experiential terms has literary but not scientific validity.

A logical empiricist may concede that thought appears to occur, but he is likely to insist that if human beings are to be studied with true scientific objectivity, most, if not all, kinds of mentalistic concepts must be ruled out. The well-known neobehaviorist B. F. Skinner, who in this regard aligns himself quite closely with logical empiricism, expresses this notion clearly when he writes:

> . . . the private event [that is, thought or consciousness] is at best no more than a link in a causal chain, and it is usually not even that. We may think before we act in the sense that we may behave covertly before we behave overtly, but our action is not an "expression" of the covert response [that is, thought] or the consequence of it. The two are attributable to the same variables.[13]

If a logical empiricist were to use the term *experience,* he would most likely define it mechanistically. To him, experience could mean no more than the conditioning process by which a person acquires a new response. If a child touches a hot stove and a link is formed between the sight of a stove and a withdrawal response, then it might be said that the child had had an experience. No thought needs to have occurred and no insights need to have been developed.

Positive relativists, however, regard experience as rooted in insightful behavior. From this point of view, experience is a psychological event which involves acting purposefully with anticipation of the probable or possible consequences of such action. Experience is interaction of a person and his perceived environment. This is what Dewey meant when he said, "An experience is always what it is because of a transaction taking place between an individual and what, *at the time,* constitutes his environment."[14] He further stated, in connection with experience and learning, that "to 'learn from experience' is to make a backward and forward connection between what we do to things and what we enjoy or suffer from things in consequence."[15] So, experience includes an active and a passive element, combined in a peculiar fashion:

> On the active hand, experience is *trying.* . . . On the passive, it is *undergoing.* When we experience something we act upon it, we do something with it; then we suffer or undergo the consequences. We do something to the thing, then it does something to us in return: such is the peculiar combination. The connection of these two phases of experience measures the fruitfulness or value of the experience. Mere activity does not constitute experience.[16]

(The word "then," as used twice in this quotation, is best interpreted to mean "at that time" or "simultaneously.")

We should note that within a positive-relativistic context the

[13] B. F. Skinner, *Science and Human Behavior* (New York: The Macmillan Company, 1953), p. 279.

[14] John Dewey, *Democracy and Education* (New York: The Macmillan Company, 1938), p. 41. (Our italics).

[15] John Dewey, *Democracy and Education* (New York: The Macmillan Company, 1916), p. 164.

[16] *Ibid.*, pp. 163–164.

present is taken to be the locus of reality. To consider anything as real is to consider it as being either in or in relation to the present. A psychological past is not merely an antecedent event. Since it is a construction within one's present life space it is to some degree and in some sense novel. As conditions or regions of the present, pasts vary as presents vary, and new pasts constantly arise. So, experience is situationally defined; it centers in neither the past nor the future, but the present. However, every experience extracts something from experiences which have gone before, modifies in some way experiences which are to follow, and influences the conditions under which future experiences may be had. Furthermore, within the experiential or perceptual process, a person is neither active nor reactive nor a combination of the two. Instead, he is *interactive,* which means that, in a perceptual or psychological situation, he simultaneously acts in relation to his psychological environment and realizes the consequences of so doing. To quote Dewey again, "An organism [person] does not live in an environment; it lives by means of an environment."[17] When one interacts with an object or activity, *he sizes it up*. Thus, a person's environment—"what is out there"—is viewed by positive relativists as fluid and dynamic, not changeless and static.

[17] John Dewey, *Logic: The Theory of Inquiry* (New York: Holt, Rinehart and Winston, Inc., 1938), p. 25.

4

WHAT IS RELATIVISTIC TRUTH AND HOW IS IT RELATED TO VALUES?

For a positive relativist, an educational philosophy should be a highly general theory that points toward the projection of large, effectual hypotheses or generalizations pertinent to education. When the hypotheses are used as plans for action, they should provide intelligent or productive directions for school personnel as they lead in a search for ways to make human life more significant and of greater worth. Hence, the ultimate test of any hypothesis—idea, principle, or generalization—is its ability to contribute to human growth. Thought functions as a guide to actions, and the result of thought is tested by its human consequences. Furthermore, a thought that has long-range ends in view involves valuation, and the exercise of this kind of thought is a characteristic that distinguishes human from subhuman activity.

Truth and values, then, are instrumental, not final; they are exposed to a continuous test of experience. The appropriateness of an act is dependent, not on some absolutistic standard, but upon the individual and group purposes and foresights which are involved in it. Through intelligent valuation, the means by which we make a living is transformed into ways of making a life that is worth the living. Positive relativism, therefore, does not involve an escape to something beyond experience, but is concerned with people's making the most and best possible growth through both personal and social experience—and growth is upward improvement from where they now are, not progress toward some ultimate, absolute perfection which transcends the workaday world.

HOW DOES A RELATIVISTIC DIFFER FROM AN ABSOLUTISTIC INTERPRETATION OF TRUTH AND VALUE?

It is in confining their philosophizing pursuits to study of interactive experiences of individuals and groups that positive relativists differ from absolutistic educational philosophers. The latter think that knowledge or truth is a final end in itself, and that nothing should be called truth unless it is either attained through the exercise of the faculties of intuition and reason (and thus independent of human experience) or is an exact experiential photographic report of existent reality.

Since an absolutist holds that truth is objective knowledge of either a metaphysical or an unlimited natural reality, an idea is true or untrue in and of itself, irrespective of its context or situation. Time and place have nothing to do with Truth. Truth, so defined, is often spelled with a capital "T" to distinguish it from the limited, functional truths of positive relativists. Although an absolutist may concede that much of the time we are guided by limited truths, which gain or lose validity according to changing circumstances, he assumes that there are at least *some* truths that are immutable and universal. Furthermore, an absolutist holds that Truth derives from sources other than man. Consequently, no matter what kinds of problems are concerned or how "human" they may seem, an absolutist does not center ultimate answers on man. Since man does not make Truth, he is obliged to try to *discover* it and live according to its dictates. So, in man's relationship to truth, man is subject and Truth is object; man proposes, but Truth disposes.

In current times, very few educational philosophers, regardless of their basic commitments, identify themselves as absolutists. Almost all of them would insist that they are tolerant of new ideas and that they recognize that man has not as yet attained the ultimate, final picture of the universe. Nevertheless, most nonrelativists are absolutistic in the sense that they either assert or assume the existence or even subsistence—transcendental existence—of an absolute universe of some kind, and they think of learning as a process of gaining more and more proximate understanding or grasp of the absolute universe. Absolutists generally recognize man's fallibility, but the very concept of fallibility implies the existence of an infallible realm of reality.

The relativism of positive relativism involves something more than a mere recognition of the possibility of illusion or error and the view that the most science can achieve is the establishment of some fairly firm probability statements within a particular context. It involves man's creating truth, not merely finding and reporting it. As positive relativists see it, any quest for the knowledge of an absolute truth is directed toward futility. For how can man know what he *would* know if he knew what he is by his very nature unequipped to know? Positive relativists therefore substitute the fruits of human interactive experience for any a priori—that is, presumptive—intuitions or operations of pure reason which would have absolute, nonempirical truth as their object. Positive relativists generally recognize that intuitive ideas concerning revealed truths and values, and the faith which they have inspired, have played an important part in Western history; but they view scientific procedures, very broadly interpreted, as now offering the best hope for man to "raise himself by his bootstraps."

The two contemporary philosophies that emphasize the value of scientific procedures are logical empiricism and positive relativism. But despite this similarity, they differ sharply regarding the light in which they place the methods of science. Whereas logical empiricists think of truth as being that which corresponds to an external, independent reality, positive relativists conceive it in terms of a human, creative interpretation of psychological reality. Truth is not, to a positive relativist, a literal description of an existence external to man. This position reflects a shift to a genuinely relativistic, scientific-reflective outlook. Such a view entails our dealing with objects relationally, rather than as things-in-themselves. Thus, it requires a distinctive method of defining truth or knowledge and an equally distinctive method of arriving at it.

In his *Logic* Dewey discussed the weaknesses of outlooks that have led into logical empiricism. It is evident that he considered these positions inferior foundations for scientific pursuits. He acknowledged the contributions of these philosophies in uprooting superstition and mysticism. However, he questioned their adequacy for modern scientific thinking.

The basic weakness of a representative of these positions, as he saw it, was this:

> It is quite willing to admit that generalizations are valid provided they have the sanction of science. But it inherited from traditional empiricism its contempt for general ideas and for theories that pretend to be anything else than summary records of ascertained facts. Its logic has no recognized place for hypotheses which at a given time outrun the scope of already determined "facts," and which, indeed, may not be capable of verification at the time or of *direct* factual verification at any time.[1]

For positive relativists, even logical principles are instrumental in nature. They are derived from whatever is involved in inquiries that have been successful. Consequently, they impose conditions to be satisfied in future inquiries until the time when the results of such inquiries show reason for modifying them.

According to positive relativism the only reality a man can ever know or work with is his own interpretation of what is real. Furthermore, since reality, relativistically defined, consists of what one gains through his five-plus senses and his manner of sizing it up, one's person is what one makes of oneself and one's environment is what one makes of that which surrounds one. A positive relativist recognizes the great difficulty, perhaps impossibility, of a person's ever getting outside himself sufficiently to make any final statements about what is absolutely real, true, or valuable. Also, he shuns the use of concepts that imply any fixed human

[1] John Dewey, *Logic: The Theory of Inquiry* (New York: Holt, Rinehart and Winston, Inc., 1938), p. 519.

traits, rigid habits of personalities, or antecedently completed reality; he always leaves the way open for genuine novelty in thought and action. Although positive relativists would not identify themselves with a revived Progressive Education movement, they do believe in, and desire, progress in our world of real risks within which men, through use of their intelligence and imagination, strive to better themselves. Man, to the best of his ability, should be the measure of all things.

The development of the notion that knowledge is a matter of human interpretation, and does not consist in a literal description of either a mentalistic or physicalistic world existing external to man, is the key contribution of positive relativism. If we assume that objects have to be dealt with relationally rather than as things-in-themselves, a distinctive method of defining truth or knowledge, and an equally distinctive process of arriving at it, are required.

Positive relativists reject the notion that man, through the use of scientific means, is able to find and use final, or absolute, truth. Consequently, they have little interest in "eternal verities." Nevertheless, they are deeply concerned with truths relativistically defined. This does not mean that they necessarily reject all absolutistic *beliefs*. But positive relativists regard knowledge as insights developed and held by human beings using human methods.

When considering their truth-value system, positive relativists think with Dewey that "the aims and ideals that move us are generated through imagination. But they are not made out of imaginary stuff. They are [human creations] made out of the hard stuff of the world of physical and social experience."[2] Accordingly, positive relativists derive a general scheme of experimental human values through experience itself, not from some set of principles which supposedly has a cosmic origin and sanction.

Absolutists tend to think in either-or categories. Consequently they tend either to reject any relational or continuum kind of thinking outright or to limit it to mundane situations of minor importance: with regard to fundamental issues there are blacks and whites but no grays. In this sort of either-or thinking we see the dominant influence of Aristotelian logic with its law of the excluded middle, stated in the formula *Either A is B or A is not B*. Such logic contrasts sharply with a relativistic experimental logic, which is concerned with treating the actual operations of human understanding in gaining truths. The logic of

[2] John Dewey, *A Common Faith* (New Haven, Conn.: Yale University Press, 1934), p. 49.

a positive relativist is not without rules, but his rules are cast within a different frame of reference, an experimental one.

Absolutistic thinking is well exemplified by the statement "A woman is either perfectly pure or she is utterly depraved; where purity is at issue, there is no middle ground." A few examples of absolutistic discontinuities are subject, or self, vs. object; reality vs. nonreality; determinism vs. free will; is's vs. ought's; behavior vs. consciousness; emotion vs. intellect; and mind vs. body. In each case one member of the discontinuity is asserted to be mutually exclusive of the other—to have nothing in common with it. But relativistically speaking, any object or idea penetrates into others to the extent of its relationships to them.

Positive relativists' approach to the achievement of knowledge or values is prospective, not retrospective. To them, predictable situational outcomes, not logical roots or historical origins as such, are what count most. Consequently, they seek insights, not into antecedent circumstances, but into contemporaneously structured experiences—life spaces. Such insights are meanings that may be considered rules for action; and meanings, at their best, are purposes abstracted and generalized so as to fit any occasion. Accordingly, a meaning is considered a rule for action, and the meaning of a statement lies in the difference it makes in purposeful operations. Thus, a statement is meaningful if it can enter into the making of a decision. Its meaning is the difference it makes for the decision. Hence, a descriptive statement is to some degree also a prescriptive one.

An idea, then, is a plan for action. A true idea is one whose consequences, when the operations which constitute its meaning are carried out, are such that they are confirmed by experience. Consequently, it helps us solve the problem in relation to which the idea was projected as a plan for action.

Since positive relativists regard truth as tentative and instrumental (not final), they refrain from making dogmatic statements about the nature of man and the universe. Rather, a statement is considered true because of its accuracy in prediction and the consensus of people competent in its area in regard to the possible consequences of acting on it—its usefulness. Nevertheless, it should be emphasized here that a relativistic definition of truth in no way discounts the value of truths. Rather, it defines truth in a more discerning manner.

Positive relativists approach both truth and value through the more or less concrete experiences of individuals. Yet interpersonal, social experiences are not overlooked. Simply stated, society is a mode of shared experience, and participation in society is one of the most important ways in which education occurs. Furthermore, every moral action is an interpersonal one. A free flow of social intercourse makes available more, and richer, experiences as a medium for judging what is true and of value. A viable culture is achieved through persons' constantly widening their participation in common interests, purposes, and values.

WHAT ARE THE MEANING AND THE SOURCE OF TRUTH?

Positive relativists strive to develop a system for establishing knowledge or truth that rests upon the most dependable methods of inquiry available. Their interpretation of the acquisition of knowledge is a description of the way problems are actually solved by scientific and reflective means. Thus, they think that "there is but one sure road of access to truth—the road of patient, coöperative inquiry operating by means of observation, experiment, record and controlled reflection."[3]

Positive-relativistic truth is an open-ended truth developed within an open system of thought. In contrast to this, an absolutist tends to set up, and fence in, knowledge with firm intellectual boundaries. At first glance, this assertion may appear contradictory to the element of limitlessness in the absolutistic position, which implies that truth, being universal and eternal, is also infinite—without boundaries. But absolute truth has very definite boundaries in the form of its adherents' nonacceptance of its being open-ended.

So absolutistic truth involves *closed* systems of meanings as contrasted with the *open* systems of positive relativism. To take an example from physics: whereas Newton's view of the universe was a closed system, the objective of a contemporary relativistic physicist is not to enclose systems of reality with unyielding boundaries, but to keep them open-ended.

For positive relativists, truths are warranted assertibilities established through man's empirical, experimental study. Truth is not inherent in ideas or objects, but is that which befalls ideas in the process of their being tested in life situations. Infor-

[3] *Ibid.*, p. 32.

mation or facts become knowledge when they are judged to be relevant to the solution of a problem, and such judgment is tested in the crucible of experience. The use of human intelligence is the best guarantee of a desirable, happy, and adequate future for men.

Positive relativists do not mean that truth has no objective standard and that it always varies from person to person, group to group, and time to time. In fact, they recognize that, fortunately, many truths have been so adequately tested that we may safely treat them as if they were certainties. However, their definition of certainty is "something in which I have tremendous faith."[4] Hence, they contend that we talk, act, and live as if we were completely confident in the reality of an existent universe—an "out-thereness"—simply because it is immensely advantageous for us to do so.

But what grounds does a positive relativist have for judging anything true? To quote Bayles, an insight is considered true "if, and only if, the deduced behavior pattern, when tested experientially or experimentally, produces the results which were anticipated."[5] Thus, an insight is true if it proves to be reasonably accurate—if what one supposes will follow from its application actually ensues. Truth, to a positive relativist, is not based upon eternal and universal principles. It is man-made, and man will change it as need be. This does not mean that truth is unimportant or ephemeral. It does mean that truth tends to evolve as human experience develops.

Within experimental logic, as contrasted with Aristotelian formal logic, thought is not a detached process carried on by a ghostlike mind, but an instrument whereby a problem that blocks some intent or purpose is resolved. Thought, then, proceeds by way of unraveling some doubt or resolving some conflict, and knowledge or truth is the outcome of thought. Thus, an interpretation of knowledge is a description of how problems are actually solved. Although in the past men have readily persuaded themselves that they were devoted to a search for intellectual certainty for its own sake, they actually sought it because of its bearing upon the preservation of what they desired and esteemed.

When truth is conceived dynamically, verification is truth mak-

[4] Hugh Skilling, "An Operational View," *American Scientists*, vol. 52, no. 4 (December 1964), p. 309A.

[5] Ernest E. Bayles, *Democratic Educational Theory* (New York: Harper & Row, Publishers, 1960), p. 113.

ing, not truth finding. Even the axioms of mathematics are postulates, creations of human thought. Furthermore, even to research scholars, facts are not "given"; they are "taken." They are constructed from controlled observations guided by hypotheses and theories. Attainment of knowledge is neither discovery nor disclosure of a predetermined reality. The very nature of the process depends upon a joint operation and achievement of a person and his environment. The human elements in knowledge can be neither completely isolated nor eliminated.

Since the basic objective of positive relativists in inquiry is not the spectatorial portrayal of some preexistent, absolute reality, but the development of instruments whereby men may more effectually find their way about in the world, their search is for the understanding of a reality which is not ultimate. Both this reality itself and their knowledge of it are experimental. Inquiry, in other words, is not a process in which spectators uncover more or less erroneously—or, in positive terms, more or less proximately—a given, fixed pre-existence or reality. In the process of their creating truth, positive relativists develop and use, not supposedly exact pictures of some absolute reality, but conceptual models. A good model is a "cognitive map" which enhances our capacity for finding our way about in the world. Since any hypothesis which explains the pertinent facts or data, or solves the problem at hand, the most successfully is regarded as true, the worth of a model consists in its aid to prediction.

Positive relativists make their models as comprehensive as possible in scope. However, they recognize that, in regard to the same general area of study, different models may be more usable for specific purposes. For instance, when one plans and makes a short trip, one uses a flat model of the earth; when the trip is much longer, one uses a spherical model; and when one is a geographer attempting an exact mathematical measurement of the earth, one's model is an oblate spheroid.

Positive relativists emphasize that our actions are based on the confidence we hold in our models. But they further note that we should not assume in such models an absolute infallibility; the range of confidence in respective models may extend from mere likelihood to certainty. However, as previously stated, certainty, experimentally defined, means extreme confidence, not absolute surety. Positive relativists recognize that there are scientific truths upon which they would stake very, very great odds. Nevertheless, they do not assume any of these to be absolute. Since the number of trials testing any truth is finite, scientific or reflective prediction or probability is likewise finite.

Everyone cannot check everything from scratch. Nevertheless, positive relativists think that it is hazardous to accept any purported truth which cannot be verified experimentally. They note that in our use of models we must give credence to the observations and findings of others who are competent in their fields of study. However, they caution that even then we should critically examine any conclusion (to the extent of our ability) to make sure that it is implicit in the pertinent data that are available.

Since knowing is neither the discovery nor the disclosure of a detached and already predetermined existence, but a process of joint inquiry involving persons and their psychological environments, relationships that are called universals are thoughts tested by their consequences and ultimately agreed upon by a community of competent knowers. Scientific study does not establish absolute inevitability, but only relative frequency and probability. So, objectivity in science means being public, not being absolute. When truth and universals are defined this way, a scientific outlook has meaning in classroom procedures as well as in scientific laboratories. In both, no special privilege need be accorded authority or tradition. The essence of a scientific outlook is devotion to empirical experimentation in a universe to which no ceiling is attributed. Free inquiry, after the pattern of scientific procedure, is therefore the most reliable road to dependable truth.

In a sense, it can be said that to scientists the experienced world is the real world, and adherents to the scientific outlook expect a scientist to accept reality unless he has grounds for withholding acceptance. But there are no strict rules to tell a scientist whether and when an apparently observed fact can or must be accepted as an objective one. There are, however, some "negative" rules which forbid the unmodified acceptance of facts that are incompatible with previously or simultaneously established truths.

Both logical empiricists and positive relativists assume that the most valid method of inquiry is scientific in nature; it is based on testable evidence. But they define "scientific method" in different ways and, as the foregoing discussion has indicated, seek different ends from it. To a positive relativist, scientific method is *not* always a sequence of steps such as a physicist supposedly uses. Scientific thinking is any form of intellectual pursuit that is based on testable evidence and is productive in relation to the goals of the thinker. To be sure, there are some measuring sticks or criteria of scientific truth; these criteria may be encompassed under the headings of adequacy and harmony in light of obtainable data. According to the principle of *adequacy*, all known pertinent facts must be taken into consideration. None may be ignored—no matter how unpalatable it might seem. Then, a conclusion, to be properly scientific, must *harmonize* all the data; that is, it must make the data add up. If a single pertinent fact seems to be contradictory, if it remains unexplained, then the conclusion is not to be trusted.

A positive relativist construes the realm of science much more broadly than does a logical empiricist. Accordingly, he assumes that scientific procedures can be applied in a very wide range of situations. He is also more flexible with respect to the kinds of data that he will consider. In psychological research, a logical empiricist is likely to admit only data of observable physical objects or substances; but a positive relativist will consider all the data of human experience, including those that may seem introspective.

Positive relativists, unlike logical positivists, do not think of science as consisting in a hierarchy—physics, chemistry, and biology at the top and education at the bottom, with psychology immediately above it. For them, each science is an area for empirical inquiry in its own right. Taking their relativism seriously, they advocate cooperation among all scientific endeavors, but do not concede that any area of science should be restricted by the specific laws, principles, concepts, and definitions of a sister science. They recognize that man may be studied in physical, biological, or psychological dimensions, and they in no way disparage the physical or biological study of man. However, they insist that to understand man's learning processes we must center our efforts on his psychological dimension. Accordingly, psychology and education should benefit from the results of scientific inquiry conducted in all areas, but they need not be bound by the constructs of any one of them.

Positive relativists extend their relativistic—open-ended—outlook to embrace all intellectual and valuational matters. Thus, they leave the way open for empirical verification of hypotheses that have previously been supported only by intuitive feelings or dogmatic beliefs, provided the hypotheses are stated in such a way as to be susceptible of verification. They recognize that, to date, no scientist as such has ascertained the absolute nature of *any* existence, either natural or supernatural. However, their minds are not closed to the possibility of a breakthrough in any of the problem areas which hitherto have been inappropriate to scientific or reflective study within the limitations of the intellectual tools at hand.

A scientific law, then, is a statement that seems true to all or most of those who are competent to study the matter. To repeat, the positive-relativistic test of truth is anticipatory accuracy, not correspondence to ultimate reality. Thus, there is a sense in which a scientific law is a generalization about which there is considerable agreement among those scientifically competent in its area; in a way, it is a matter of consensus. The test of its validity, however, is not this consensus but the law's predictive accuracy. Positive relativists assume that no scientific law is "sacred"; any law may change, and indeed over the course of time most will. A significant aspect of their thinking is the expectation of change. They are much more likely than logical empiricists to think of both nature and culture as undergoing continuous modification.

By the very nature of positive relativism, scientific generalizations, of whatever kind, do not advance beyond the realm of the hypothetical—seems as if. However, hypotheses may be verified to the point at which we may safely treat them as if they were absolute:

> Relativistically speaking, the world's wisdom is taken to be couched in the form of hypotheses, free inventions of human minds, hypotheses in which greater or lesser degrees of assurance can be placed, dependent upon their degree of verification by human experience particularly in the form of scientific experimentation.[6]

HOW IS TRUTH RELATED TO VALUES?

Traditional absolutistic thinking has tended to erect a wall of total separation between facts and values. For example, logical empiricists think of facts as purely a product of the empirical reporting of observations based strictly on sensory data, and hence completely objective. They then think of values as subjective and personal. Consequently, whereas in the realm of facts they hold to a rigid determinism, in regard to values they emphasize all-out personal autonomy.

[6] Carl G. Hempel, "The Logical Analysis of Psychology," in *Readings in Philosophical Analysis*, Herbert Feigl and Wilfred Sellars, eds. (New York: Appleton-Century-Crofts, 1949), p. 378.

In contrast to logical empiricists, positive relativists see values arising within the course of human experience, and their development's being amenable to the same type of intellectual procedures that characterize scientific inquiry. Thus, human values do not proceed from a supernatural realm, but neither are they merely expedient, whimsical feelings that have no relationship to verified knowledge. Reflective scientific procedures is the supreme means of valid determination in all aspects of human—personal-social—living.

Science itself is a value in that it is the expression and fullfillment of a special human desire and interest. Any scientist, even when he is being a scientist, exercises his feelings to some degree. So, any experience of thinking has its own aesthetic qualities. Thinking rarely if ever occurs apart from feeling. A person who habitually exercises a high level of intelligence also experiences much emotion or feeling as he thinks. So emotion is one aspect of the process we call thinking. Of course, some types of feeling, if experienced with intensity, may hinder rational decision. One of the most common is the fear a person feels when he thinks some aspect of his self is under threat. However, the most careful thought may be accompanied by considerable amounts of fear, discouragement, elation, or other feeling states.

> Only the psychology that has separated things which in reality belong together holds that scientists and philosophers think while poets and painters follow their feelings. In both, and to the same extent in the degree in which they are of comparable rank, there is emotionalized thinking, and there are feelings whose substance consists of appreciated meanings or ideas.[7]

Whereas logical empiricists would revel in Einstein's statement that "for the scientist, there is only 'being,' but no wishing, no valuing, no good, no evil—in short, no goal,"[8] positive relativists would read further, to where Einstein wrote, "Ethical axioms are found and tested not very differently from the axioms of science. . . . Truth is what stands the test of experience."[9]

Important scientific discoveries of recent centuries were not made simply by piling facts upon facts. Rather, they were made through scientists' perceptions of the significant relationships or

[7] John Dewey, *Art as Experience* (New York: G. P. Putnam's Sons, 1934), p. 73.

[8] Philipp Frank, *Relativity a Richer Truth* (Boston: Beacon Press, 1950), "Foreword by Albert Einstein," p. vi.

[9] *Ibid.*, p. vii.

the meaningful patterns among facts. The essence of a viable scientific process is this: When, in relation to a problem, we are confronted with alternative or conflicting views, hypotheses, or propositions, we should ask what they mean, what considerations and evidence support them, what evidence speaks against them, and which alternative is more plausible or tenable in light of all available pertinent information.

The same general *pattern* of inquiry (not necessarily the same specific methods and techniques) that is followed in the resolution of conflicts of knowledge in scientific disciplines can and should be used to establish effective value judgments. Everything, including values, should be judged by its consequences in and on human experience. When value judgments issue from reflective inquiry, they too are public, shared, warranted assertibilities. So positive relativists move evaluation from the domain of supernatural intuitiveness to a scientific context. The process of evaluation (i.e., of arriving at a conclusion about the merits of a value) is an epistemological—knowledge getting—process involving very much the same techniques as a scientific inquiry to establish the tenability of a generalization in regard to "factual" matters.

Through an understanding of the positive-relativistic interpretation of experience and reality within which intellectual and emotional factors are interwoven, truth and value acquire a joint meaning that gives a continuity of cognitive and evaluational functions. Accordingly, positive relativists contend that ethical and artistic values, like intellectual ones, can be warranted assertibilities resulting from inquiry and reflection. Thus, for them there is no sharp cleavage between precisely defined areas of scientific confirmation and evaluational endeavors; all worthy ideas or propositions are construed as instruments for human progress that may be established through reflective processes. We should, therefore, center our thinking on the use that is to be made of ideas and objects either now or in the future. Although positive relativists agree that probably no single criterion of value can be devised for all societies and cultures, they do not infer from this that we should subscribe to moral or valuational anarchy.

In summarizing the relationship between scientific knowledge and artistic values, we may say that although there is a necessary distinction between the two, under human direction there should be no real opposition between them. When we take the idea of science broadly, we place emphasis upon scientific *methods* of inquiry which enable us to gather facts effectively and use them more intelligently. These methods center upon a steady, cumulative growth of insights, which gives us a constantly enlarging power of human direction. Original and daring creations of artistic individuals are achieved, not by the artists' ignoring science, but by their making new integrations of scientifically established knowledge. Thus, in a real sense, the increasing command of scientific methods and coordinate systematized subject matter truly liberates people.

WHAT ARE THE NATURE AND THE SOURCE OF VALUES?

Simply stated, values consist of what we prize or are willing to settle for. However, immediate likings, enjoyments, or desires are not in themselves values; they provide problematic material for the construction of values. Likings are often associated with values, but they become values only when they are judgmentally approved. Some "natural" likings become ends to be sought, whereas others are ends to be rejected.

Evaluative appreciation is a process of appraisal—determination of both positive and negative qualities of an activity. To appreciate something, one need not necessarily like it. To have positive value, an object or activity must be desired, but its being desired is only a necessary condition, not a sufficient one, for its being valuable; the object or activity, in addition to being desired, must be desirable.

The problem of valuation is then, How do we test the desirability of a desired function? Basically, positive relativists do this by noting the conditions out of which an activity has grown, the circumstances that surround it, and the consequences that are either likely or certain to follow from its performance. Although they have no single criterion of value, they in no way endorse moral anarchy. It is not a case of "everything goes." Some values really have validity. Furthermore, values are not equally acceptable, but their acceptability is not determined by resorting to an absolutistic source. Thus, positive relativists bypass absolutes in values or morality as well as in the goals of science.

Morality and values, as developed in schools, should be independent of any specific theological foundation. However, this does not mean that a student's interlacing of values and theology should be belittled by his school. But in school, the students and teacher should approach valuation by using the tools of human intelligence and invention. In this way, they will shift the center of gravity of morality from theological doctrine to personal-social relations. Any absolutistic approach to valuation tends to place values in the hands of a minority—the human authority for the absolutistic value. Such valuation is usually not in the best interests of the majority. Positive relativists are committed to the position that genuine values do not exist apart from the desires of persons. Nor can a set of supremely good and desirable values be determined intellectually by *discovering inherent* purposes, goals, or functions of life disassociated from any specific persons. More precisely stated, they posit no a priori, standardized, rational principles upon which morals or values rest. Values do not *inhere* in objects, activities, persons, or anything else; they arise through intelligent relationships of persons with other persons and with objects around them.

Experience is capable of developing its own regulative standards. So, ends should be framed in terms of the possibilities of actual experiential situations. Even our most basic ideals and ends should be shaped as hypotheses to provide satisfaction for human needs and desires. Values, then, are relative, not absolute; they are relative to developing human needs and desires, reflectively evaluated within an individual-social context. A concept of value confined to any one individual in his several but isolated natures is quite meaningless; values are personal-social, not individual as such. Furthermore, values should be developed through the process of reflective study within which all considerations, scientific or otherwise, pertinent to the matter at hand and obtainable under the prevailing circumstances are taken into account.

For logical empiricists, whereas facts are descriptive of an independently existing reality, values are only normative; that is, either they are subjective, emotional matters of wish or they are absolute, nonempirical pronouncements. In neither case are they amenable to empirical study, and they are therefore removed from any sort of scientific inquiry. To logical empiricists there is no way of bridging the gap—no argument capable of advancing logically—from an "is" premise in regard to reality to an "ought" conclusion, which is normative and prospective.

Positive relativists grant that an inference from "is" to "ought" cannot validly be drawn within Aristotelian formal logic, but all that is indicated by this is the inadequacy of absolutistic logic, an inadequacy which stems from the assertion of sharp discontinuities between concepts of factual matters and concepts of ideals. Some logical-empiricistic discontinuities related to evaluation are behavior vs. consciousness, body vs. mind, intellect vs. emotion, factual vs. aesthetic, and science vs. art.

For positive relativists, evaluation at its best is neither a whimsical process nor a narrowly prejudiced one. Rather, it is a process that is reflective, deliberate, and comprehensive. Values are of human origin, and absolute values as such are unobtainable; a value always exists in relation to people and other values. So, normative standards should be grounded in reflective empirical inquiry of an experimental nature. In the evaluative process, honest, careful deliberation pointed toward desirable actions is set over against either people's conformance to set standards or their basing their activity on mere good intentions or natural proclivities. Traditional moral standards of a culture are not in themselves rules for living, but hypotheses to be tested. Learned moral responsibility means ability and willingness to predict and deliberately intend certain acts and their consequences. People should evaluate their actions in terms of their lasting, long-range, satisfying consequences contrasted with the probable results of any known possible alternative actions.

Values, then, are instrumental, not ultimate or final, and man is the originator, conservator, and changer of his values. Values are closely related to the world in which we find ourselves. What count are the foreseeable consequences of a proposed line of conduct, in terms of their bearing on human relations. Values center upon men's preservation and enhancement of selves both individually and collectively, and there is no necessary conflict between the two. Enhancement of individuals and enhancement of groups to which they belong are complementary processes.

Values arise within the stream of experience, and there is an aspect of value in every experience from that of loving someone to that of gaining an understanding of the most abstract mathematical formula. All conduct that is not either blindly impulsive or mechanically routine involves valuation. "The problem of valuation is thus closely associated with the problem of the structure of the sciences of *human* activities and *human* relations."[10]

Positive relativism is melioristic in regard to values as well as knowledge. *Meliorism* signifies the outlook that matters can be constantly improved through learning, so we always should strive

[10] John Dewey, *Theory of Valuation* (Chicago: The University of Chicago Press, 1939), p. 3.

to make them better. Progress centers upon increased meaning of current continuous experiences of perceptually interactive persons. So progress is most dependably achieved through our extension of the significance of ourselves and our environments as we experience them.

Positive relativists think that *better* is more worthy than *best*. So, it is better to travel than to arrive. But, in a sense, traveling is a constant arriving. However, one's arrival should never preclude further traveling. An arrival that precluded more traveling would imply that one was either asleep or dead. For positive relativists, therefore, ends in view, when reached, become means in a continuing experiential process. Growth—"traveling"—cuts across any ends-means discontinuity. Growth is not a means to any ultimate or final end, but only to more growth. Moreover, we may grow upward from where we now are without there being a bench mark on an absolute ceiling toward which we are shooting.

Since positive relativists do not evaluate attitudes and actions on a metaphysical basis, they consider them valuable or virtuous when they reflect (1) confidence in the continued development of truth through directed, cooperative human endeavor; (2) devotion to experimental study in an open-ended universe that is given no ceiling; (3) pursuance, even against obstacles, of activities in behalf of ideal ends because of the conviction of their general and enduring value; (4) expansion and enrichment of ideals and application of the ideals to actual life and growth; (5) development of richer selves in terms of insights, goals, ideals, and interests that provide a pattern of objectives for the improvement of personal-social living; and (6) acquisition of deep, enduring dynamic adaptations in life.

The sixth criterion involves something other than a continuous state of contentment. A moral life implies involvement and even perplexity. Enduring dynamic adaptations entail a process of living within which persons effectually rework or reconstruct both themselves and their environments so as to reach goals that they consider important in light of the purposes they are pursuing.

Our observation of these criteria of value would mean our commitment to a democratic way of life. However, the commitment would be of such nature as not to elevate democracy to the position of an absolute. Democracy, as positive relativists see it, represents the best insights that men have, to date, about what is required for the fullest development of individuals and society. The distinctive characteristic that prevents democracy from becoming absolutistic is its inherent principle that, whenever human insight is improved, human standards will vary accordingly. As intellectual development proceeds, such variation may possibly come to replace the very principles of democracy with something better. In their broader sense, democratic principles apply to all phases of human activity. They entail a continuous extension of common interests and purposes among men, despite their differences, as they construct a way to a better life. (See pages 100–103 for a positive-relativistic characterization of democracy and its leadership.)

5

FOR POSITIVE RELATIVISTS, WHAT IS LEARNING?

Maturation or learning, or a combination of the two, is the means by which lasting changes in persons occur. Maturation is a developmental process within which a person from time to time manifests different traits, the "blueprints" for which have been carried in his cells from the time of his conception. Learning, in contrast with maturation, is any enduring change in a living individual which is not heralded by his genetic inheritance.

Since teachers can do little to influence the maturational patterns of students, except perhaps to accelerate or retard them to some degree, their most effectual area of endeavor always centers upon learning. Furthermore, because of man's unique traits and capacities, learning is far more crucial to him than it is to the lower animals.

There is apparently no group of human beings that has not, through learning, developed some devices for enriching its contacts with the world about it. In the development of these devices, people have attempted to derive satisfactions from understanding and manipulating their world as well as through merely touching, smelling, and tasting its various aspects. Moreover, contrasted with the capacities of less advanced animals, man's potential for becoming human lies in his capacity to extend his learning experience to a world of symbolism and thereby to operate on various levels of reality.

An integral part of a systematic educational philosophy is its approach to, and understanding of, the learning process. Everyone who either teaches or expects to teach has a theory of learning as well as a philosophy of education. A teacher may be able to describe his theory in explicit terms or he may not. However, in either case one can usually deduce the basic nature of a teacher's theory from his actions. The important question therefore involves not whether a teacher has a theory of learning, but rather how tenable his theory seems to be.

Everything a teacher does is colored by the theory he holds. Consequently, a teacher who does not make use of a systematic body of psychological as well as philosophical theory in his day-by-day decisions is behaving blindly. Hence, little evidence of a long-range rationale, purpose, or plan is observable in his teaching. A teacher without a strong theoretical orientation inescapably makes little more than busywork assignments. True, many teachers operate this way and use only a hodgepodge of methods without any systematic theoretical orientation. However, this muddled kind of teaching is undoubtedly responsible for many of the current adverse criticisms of public education.

But a teacher need not base his thinking on tradition and folklore. Instead, he may be quite aware of the most important theories developed by professional educational psychologists and philosophers—in which case his own theory is likely to be quite sophisticated. As we stated in Chapter 2, a positive relativistic educational philosophy implies a cognitive-field psychology of learning. The present chapter concentrates on a description and explanation of this psychological position as it relates particularly to the learning process.

The constructs and methodology of cognitive-field psychology serve a positive-relativistic outlook very well in that they constitute an advantageous instrument for the establishment of warranted assertibilities concerning human, intelligent behavior and learning. Contrariwise, they are not designed to provide a means for any spectatorial report in regard to some absolute human existence in terms of fixed natural laws and cause-effect necessities.

Learning, relativistically conceived, is the process whereby a psychological person emerges and grows. Thus, it is that procedure whereby an individual with a unique type of biological organism lives in a human society and becomes a human—cultural—being. Whereas from the viewpoint of biology a man is a physical organism, psychologically he is a dynamic person who emerges within a social environment.

Learning or psychological development has no necessary one-to-one relationship to physical or biological behavior or change. A child's becoming larger is biological growth, and his being moved from a theater to his home while he is sleeping constitutes physical movement; but neither represents psychological development. A person's learning or psychological development cannot be ascertained merely through direct observation; it must be *inferred* through observation and study of his total situation. A total psychological situation is a *life space* or a *psychological field*.

Positive-relativistic cognitive-field theory contrasts sharply with the logical-empiricistic behaviorisms or conditioning theories (these latter two have synonymous meanings) in regard to the manner in which adherents of the two respective positions use observable behavior of persons as psychological data. Behaviorists use observable behavior and only observable behavior as data. Consequently, they restrict learning objectives to those expressible in terms of observable behaviors. In contrast, cognitive-field psychologists, although they also study observable behaviors, infer from these data the changing personalities, environments, and insights of the persons being studied. So, whereas for behaviorists one's physical behavior is also one's psychological behavior, for cognitive-field theorists psychological behavior is something quite different from mere physical movement; it is change in the way a person perceives both himself and his psychological environment.

For positive relativists, all forms of learning have a common element; they all involve change in an individual's experiential situation that gives him an expectation of greater control in regard to matters involved in his current and subsequent experience. A person learns through his reconstruction of experience, through making a backward and forward connection between what he does with things around him and the consequences he enjoys or suffers as a result of dealing with them.

Knowledge, the product of learning, is gained through experience. It is concerned, not with either antecedent or ultimate reality, but with the effective direction of human activity in relation to perceived reality. The conception of a priori knowledge—knowledge independent of human experience—is rather meaningless; knowledge is a goal within inquiry, not an end outside or beyond it. Furthermore, there is a continuity of viability in all forms of knowledge from the most abstract science of mathematics to the art of manual labor.

At this point, the reader is advised to review Chapter 2, which provides background information for the remaining sections of the current chapter.

HOW IS LEARNING A PURPOSIVE PROCESS?

The way positive relativism differs from logical empiricism becomes more vivid when we appraise the assumptions that undergird the respective psychologies of learning that are most germane to each educational philosophy. Logical empiricists manifest a preference for assuming passivity on the part of men, therefore they attack assumptions which they think imply in human beings a basically active nature. Accordingly, they have a strong affinity for behavioristic or conditioning psychologies and often attack cognitive-field psychological approaches by (erroneously) attributing to them the promotion of the concepts of innate human activity and autonomous intuitive awareness.

Cognitive-field psychology promotes the idea of man's being purposively, perceptually interactive, but it in no way sponsors the concepts of autonomous human activity or natural unfoldment. Its being a purposive psychology involves the assumption that intellectual processes are deeply affected by an individual's goals and that learning activity, including habit formation, is goal-directed. Accordingly, ideas concerning goals or purposes become central to cognitive-field learning theory. This contrasts sharply with the practices of adherents of conditioning theories, who either ignore learners' goals or purposes completely or make them only peripheral and incidental.

Logical empiricists and behavioristic psychologists tend to consider any concept of goal direction or purposiveness to be teleological—supernaturally designed. To them "teleological" means deriving man's present behavior from the future; consequently, it sounds mystical and superstitious. So, in their zeal to escape any commitment to the view that the future has a bearing on causation, they have emphasized past events as the cause of present behavior. Whereas logical-empiricistic behaviorists center the understanding of an individual in his past pointed toward the present, positive relativists, and likewise cognitive-field theorists, center their study of an individual in the present projected into the future.

The purposive nature of learning, which positive relativists emphasize, is within, not outside, the stream of contemporaneous experience. Thus it is not teleological. Still, there are at least three levels of such purposiveness. One level, which is shared with lower animals, appears to be simply the maintenance of normalcy. As John F. Dashiell put it, "Through all animal life an outstanding characteristic runs—the tendency of the organism to maintain its normalcy against internal or external disrupting agencies."[1] This characteristic often is referred to as *homeostasis,* a term popularized by Walter Cannon earlier in the century.[2] Examples of homeostasis are found in the way an organism fights disease without aid of medicine, or the ways in which wounds heal, broken bones knit, or a kidney increases its functioning to compensate for the loss of its twin.

The other two levels of nonteleological purposiveness involve (1) biological organisms and (2) psychological persons in relation to their respective environments. As defined by Cannon, homeostasis is the process by which a disturbed organism tends to eliminate the disturbance and return to its former state. However, C. A. Mace has developed some extensions of the original theory. He has suggested that, in homeostasis, what is maintained or restored is not so much an internal state of an organism, although to a degree this does happen, but more a satisfactory

[1] Quoted in Arthur W. Combs and Donald Snygg, *Individual Behavior,* rev. ed. (New York: Harper & Row, Publishers, 1959), p. 41.

[2] See Walter Cannon, *The Wisdom of the Body* (New York: W. W. Norton & Company, Inc., 1932) for many excellent examples of homeostasis at work.

relation of the organism and its environment. Moreover, a specific equilibrium is rarely maintained, so it is better to refer to the attainment of new equilibriums rather than merely to the restoration of previous ones.[3]

Positive relativists, in embracing cognitive-field psychology, extend the concepts of purposiveness and homeostasis to a psychological domain. Psychologically, a person strives to effect new equilibriums between himself and his psychological environment throughout his continuous series of overlapping life spaces. It is within this purposive process that psychological needs emerge, and it is in relation to such needs that learning—psychological growth—occurs.

Man is born a very complex biological organism in a social environment. Throughout his waking hours, as a baby, later as a child, and then as a youth, he learns by trying various acts and seeing what happens. Thus, through his purposive living in a human environment, an individual develops as a person or self. A normal process of development produces self-involvement with objects, people, groups, and social organizations. In a negative sense, a human organism growing up in complete isolation would probably not develop a self-concept or appear to others as a personality. It seems reasonable to assume that he would have no basis for distinguishing right from wrong, no developed aesthetic sense, and no use of language or symbols. Consequently, he would be incapable of abstract thinking. Only by living in a human world and having a biological organism of a unique type does a biological man emerge as a psychological person, or self. The form that the development of selfhood takes depends upon the learning that results from the purposive interaction of the person and his psychological environment.

Conditioning theorists in the logical-empiricist tradition make much of pleasure and pain, or satisfaction and annoyance, as instigators of behavior. An organism is presumably so constructed biologically as to seek pleasurable states and avoid painful ones. Constrastedly, cognitive-field psychologists are more likely to talk about success and failure as motivators, the former being truly a reward for completing an act.

Success and failure are not merely achievements as such but represent the relationship between a person's ambitions and his achievements. If he has a certain level of aspiration and is able

[3] C. A. Mace, "Homeostasis, Needs and Values," *British Journal of Psychology*, August 1953, p. 3.

to achieve this level, he feels good about it. If he attains success at one level of aspiration, he is likely to raise the level, and to continue doing so as long as he is able to perform successfully. Thus, goals tend to be more self- than environment-centered and to change in dynamic fashion with each new experience.

A person's perceptions, attitudes, and prejudices are learned significances for guidance of purposive behavior. One creates or develops these significances or expectations in order to act effectively, and one is unlikely to alter them unless and until either one's actions are blocked or one's purposes are changed. So, cognitive-field psychologists are convinced that psychological activity depends upon energy related to psychological tension systems. Accordingly, they emphasize that learning is associated with changes in the valences—values—of aspects of a person and his psychological environment and changes in tension systems of the person in relation to regions of this environment.

WHAT IS THE COGNITIVE-FIELD THEORY OF LEARNING?

The cognitive-field psychology of learning has been formulated in an attempt to construct a scientific psychology of learning highly applicable to classroom situations. Positive relativists rest its validity upon educational results, scientifically ascertained. They are convinced that, in light of the present stage of scientific development, this theory of learning is more likely than any other of which they are aware to lead to the most productive results in classroom procedures.

Whereas behavioristic educational psychologies have emphasized overt behavior, cognitive-field psychology concerns itself with outward behavior only insofar as it may provide clues to what is transpiring psychologically or perceptually. Thus, *psychological* is understood to mean in accordance with the logic of a growing mind or intelligence. To be psychological in his pursuits, a cognitive-field psychologist must therefore look at the world through the eyes of the learner. To describe a situation psychologically, he must, to the best of his ability, describe the situation that confronts the individual under study. Such a situation is viewed as a pattern of person-environmental relationships that provide and limit opportunity. Once the person-environmental structure is established, the problem is to use constructs and methods adequate to deal with the underlying dynamics of behavior and to do this in a scientifically sound manner.

Cognitive-field psychology describes how a person gains understanding of himself and his world in a situation within which his self and his environment compose a totality of mutually interdependent, coexisting events. This psychology involves the kind of generalizations about learning that may be applied to actual persons in school situations. It is associated with the knowing and understanding functions which give meaning to a situation. Also, it is built around the purposes underlying behavior, the goals involved in behavior, and persons's means and processes of understanding themselves as they function in relation to their goals. Factors of a life space acquire meaning as a person formulates his goals and develops insights into ways of achieving them.

A functional interpretation of psychological life opens the way for extensive use of systematic constructs. Whereas a behaviorist supposedly restricts his generalizations to those based on the use of "objective" data, a cognitive-field psychologist knowingly uses constructs that go beyond the observable data. His employment of such constructs provides a means of bridging the gap between general laws, which cannot be observed, and the functions of individual persons, which can be gathered as data. Thus, through the use of a few constructs the essence of an individual case can be adequately represented.

A *construct* is an invented idea.[4] It is a generalized concept not directly observable but formed from data that are observed. Its purpose is to correlate a broad range of data which have some basic functional similarity, despite their marked superficial differences. A need, psychologically defined, is an example of a construct. Since it has no length, breadth, thickness, or mass, it cannot be observed. Yet it is a crucial, functional concept in studying human activity. The *meaning of all the constructs of cognitive-field psychology are mutually interdependent*. Each depends for its meaning upon the meanings of all the others. Thus, there are no independent, dependent, and intervening variables, as in the behaviorisms. Instead, *all the variable of cognitive-field psychology are interdependent.*

[4] See Morris L. Bigge and Maurice P. Hunt, *Psychological Foundations of Education*, 2nd ed. (New York: Harper & Row, Publishers, 1968), pp. 380–386, for descriptions of the key constructs of cognitive-field psychology.

HOW DOES COGNITIVE-FIELD LEARNING THEORY WORK?

The cognitive-field theory of learning is closely related to, and derived from, *cognitive* and *field* psychological theories.[5] *Cognitive* is derived from the Latin verb *cognoscere,* which means "to know." Cognitive theory deals with the problem of how people gain an understanding of themselves and their environments and how, using their cognitions, they act in relation to their environments. A *field* consists of the concurrent interrelationships in any one situation. Field theory in psychology centers on the idea that all psychological activity of a person, at a given juncture, occurs in a field. Such activity is a function of a totality of coexisting factors, which are mutually interdependent.

A field situation is perceived in such a way that any change in the field depends upon the nature of the field at that time. An astronomer uses "field" to describe the universe and predict the orbits of stars. A biologist relates the function of cells to their location in a growth "field." A physicist uses "field" in his study of the structure of an atom. Similarly, a psychologist uses "field" to mean the total psychological world in which a person lives at a given time. It includes a psychological past, present, and future, also a concrete and imaginative reality—all interpreted as simultaneous aspects of a current situation. An individual's understanding of his field—his learning—is his *insight* into, or *cognitive structure* of, his life space.

What is insight or cognitive structure?

Insight, concisely defined, is a basic sense of, or feeling for, relationships. Thus, it is either a particularized or generalized meaning or discernment. A generalized insight is an understanding.

Although there is nothing about the term *insight* that requires it to be right in any absolutistic sense, it is a grasp of a situation that often does go deeper than words. Thus, it is a realizing sense of a matter. So, insight into a situation is its meaning. Meaning, so used, denotes that to which an object or idea points or what it signifies. The insights of a person are not equated with his consciousness or awareness or his ability to describe them verbally;

[5] See Gardner Lindzey and Elliott Aronson, *The Handbook of Social Psychology*, 2nd ed., vol. 1 (Reading, Mass.: Addison-Wesley Publishing Co., Inc. 1968), chaps. 5 and 6.

instead, their essence is a sense of, or feeling for, pattern in a life situation.

Development of insight means getting the feel of, grasping the idea of, catching on to, or seeing through a situation. An insight is acquired through one's actually or symbolically doing something and seeing what happens. The focus of the learning is on the seeing, not (as has been assumed by behaviorists) on the doing. Seeing, here, is broadly defined to mean catching the point or getting the idea. Any or all of the senses, however many these may be, may be involved, and the sensory action may be pronounced, or it may be so rudimentary that the person involved may not realize it is occurring. Thus, he may think he is learning through his "mind's eye."

A person may gain an insight through experiencing only one case. However, the most valuable insights are those confirmed by enough similar cases to be generalized into an understanding. A generalized insight or an understanding is a meaning or discernment that one may apply to several or even many similar, but not necessarily identical, situations or processes.

A person's insights collectively constitute the cognitive structure of his life space. However, the term *insight* is also sometimes used in a generic sense. Thus, the two expressions *insight* and *cognitive structure* may be considered synonyms. *Cognitive structure* means the way a person perceives the psychological aspect of his personal, physical, and social world. Such a world includes a person and all of his facts, concepts, beliefs, memory traces, and expectations. Consequently, changes in the cognitive structure of life spaces prevail in the development of language, emotions, attitudes, actions, and social interrelations.

How do cognitive-field theorists use the life-space concept?

Within cognitive-field psychology, life space is a model of psychological reality or functional relationships developed for the purpose of describing both what is possible and what is impossible for the person being studied, and anticipating or predicting what he is likely to be thinking and doing now as well as what his subsequent thoughts and actions will be (see Figure 3). So, in psychological study, one starts with a model of a person and the world around him as it is pertinent to that person. Learning is a modification of the person's world as represented by the model. Life space—the psychological model—contains the person himself, the goals he is seeking, the negative "goals" he is attempting to avoid, the barriers

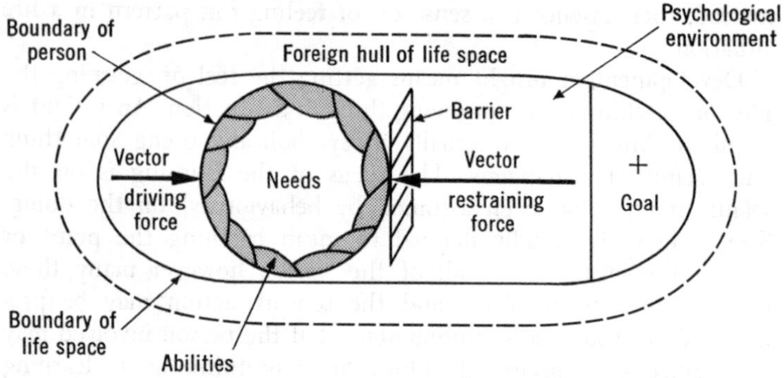

FIGURE 3. Life space, the psychological model.

between himself and his goals which restrict his psychological movement toward them, and the paths—both potential and actual—to his goals. Psychological paths are ways of achieving goals.

The two principal aspects of a life space are a person and his psychological environment. The two are not mutually exclusive; however, they function as sub-wholes of the psychological field—life space. Both are surrounded by a nonpsychological foreign hull. A person is a consciously behaving functional self, which is evidenced through the individual's abilities and needs. A person's psychological environment consists of everything in which, toward which, or away from which he can make psychological movement—do anything about.

A foreign hull is composed of those aspects of an organism's physical and social environment which are observable by the one studying the particular person but at that moment have no significance for the person being studied. Thus, it is the complex of all nonpsychological factors surrounding a life space. It is made up of physical and social factors that, at the time being considered, are not subject to a person's psychological conceptualization, but that may, at any future time, become parts of his psychological field. Thus, a person's foreign hull constitutes the outer limits of his behavioral possibilities. However, a person can never experience any aspect of his own foreign hull; when he experiences a part of his previous foreign hull, it is no longer a part of his present foreign hull but belongs to his life space proper.

In a life space, a person and his psychological environment are in simultaneous mutual interaction (SMI) and are mutually interdependent. Each depends upon the other for its nature and functions; it is impossible to treat one adequately without also treating the other. Accordingly, one's person is definitive of one's environment and likewise one's environment is definitive of oneself. Usually, a series of a person's continuous, overlapping life spaces, each consisting of the person and the respective environment of the moment, are reasonably similar. They are not, however, identical. Each, to some degree, is different from the one that preceded it and the one that follows. Since we can anticipate some degree of similarity and continuity of life spaces as the experiences of one moment shade into those of the next, for practical schoolroom procedures, depending upon the purposes being pursued, we may assume a fixity of life spaces for longer periods than a moment—perhaps a class period, a week, or a month.

Within a series of overlapping life spaces, a person's life is a continuity of psychological tensions, locomotions, and new equilibriums. When there is an increase of tension in one part of a life space relative to the rest of the system, disequilibrium occurs. When a person finds himself in a state of disequilibrium and attempts to return to equilibrium, psychic energy is expended; he engages in psychological behavior or locomotion. Should tension throughout the system become completely equalized, output of energy would cease; the total system would come to rest. Of course, throughout a life span this absolute balance is never achieved. Since a person is intelligent and purposive, he constantly expands and restructures his life space to some degree; consequently, new disequilibriums continuously emerge. This process gives a dynamic nature to human living that makes it immensely interesting and challenging.

Nonpsychological factors observed only by an outsider can at the next moment become psychological ones for the person being studied. A prime characteristic of the parts of a life space and their regions is their permeability. There can be movement both ways through the boundary of a person of a life space or through the boundaries of any of their regions. Aspects of self may move into future environmental regions of the life space or even into the foreign hull, and vice versa. Only the inner stratum of self—needs—remains relatively stable, although it too may change drastically over periods of time, as when a person changes his religious faith.

Since succeeding nonpsychological physical and social environments—foreign hulls—are outside psychological environments,

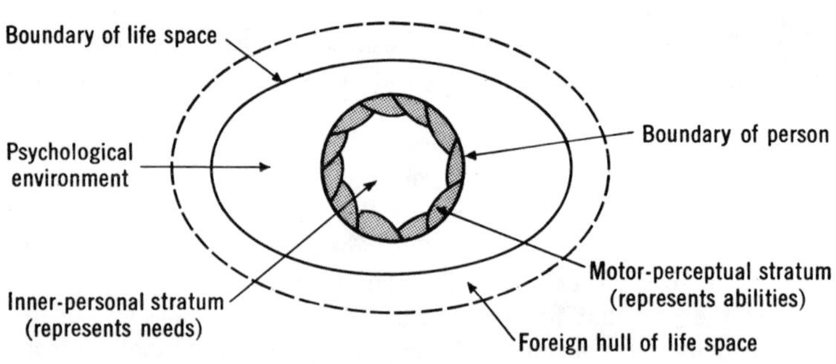

FIGURE 4. A structured person in a life space.

they can have no immediate effect upon a person's intelligent behavior. However, through a person's interaction with his environment, parts of a present foreign hull are transformed into goals, barriers, and other psychological factors of future life spaces. They then are no longer a part of the foreign hull. Factors thus transformed become parts of subsequent psychological environments. Thus, what a moment before constituted only a part of the foreign hull may at the succeeding moment be a central part of the person or his psychological environment.

A person may be represented as a differentiated region of a life space (see Figure 4). The field of a newborn baby is something like "one big blooming buzzing confusion." Then, as he lives his life, although he may not think of it in these specific terms, his total situation is structured as his *self*—person—and his *environment*. Some aspects of experience involve the central core of a person; they are very near and dear to him. Others are of a less vital, peripheral sort. Hence, we may think of a person as structured into outer and inner layers. Some experiences involve only the more peripheral areas, whereas others embrace the most central regions of a psychological person.

Psychologically, a person is composed of (1) a motor-perceptual stratum (region) and (2) an inner-personal stratum (region). The motor-perceptual stratum has the position of a boundary zone between the inner-personal region and the environment. It represents the knowing and manipulative abilities of a person. *Motor-perceptual system* denotes the phenomenon which a behaviorist would see simply as body or organism. In a sense, the motor-perceptual system is the tool of the inner-personal system. Like regions of the psychological environment, it provides opportunity

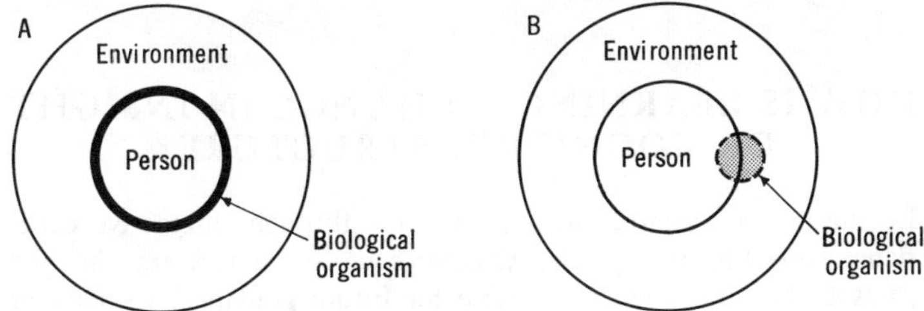

FIGURE 5. Relationship of a biological organism to a psychological person.

and limits opportunity. However, it is more closely identified with the self than with the environment.

Whereas abilities are centered in the motor-perceptual system, needs are centered in the inner-personal system. A *need* is a state of a person that has a part in determining behavior toward any goals that may exist in relation to that state; it corresponds to a personal tension. Since the motor-perceptual region is functionally located between the inner-personal region and the environment, it performs functions of both person and environment. This means that a person acts in relation to his environment and simultaneously realizes the consequences of so doing.

Is an organism person or environment?

In a relativistic sense, an organism is an aspect of both the person and his psychological environment.. A person usually identifies his biological organism closely with himself. But he also sees his organism in another light as an important aspect of his environment; it is part of that with which he must learn to live. A child's or youth's being crippled, or abnormal in physical size or proportions, may color everything he says or does. A 12-year-old girl who reaches the adolescent growth spurt early and becomes head and shoulders taller than any other student in her class may consider her physical stature a critical aspect of her psychological environment; she must live with what she "makes of" her physical stature.

We may illustrate the relation of a biological organism to a person in two different ways. The organism may be considered a boundary region of a person which mediates between the person and his environment by providing cognitive and manipulative abilities (Figure 5A), or the functions of the organism may be pictured as a factor common to both a psychological person and his psychological environment (Figure 5B).

HOW IS LEARNING A CHANGE IN INSIGHT OR COGNITIVE STRUCTURE?

Learning is a dynamic process whereby, through interactive experience, insights or cognitive structures of life spaces are changed so as to become more serviceable for future guidance. Insights or cognitive structure are answers to questions concerning such matters as how something is made up, what one belongs to, how one does something, of what good a thing or an action is, and what one should be doing. They may be verbal, preverbal, or nonverbal. One may gain an insight before one has words to express it, one may have a complete and exact verbalization involving no or little insight, or the insight and the verbalization may be achieved simultaneously. There is evidence that even nonverbal animals solve mazes by formulating a series of cognitive structures and testing them, and that they solve their problems through gaining insight into their situations.[6] What occurs psychologically when, by being given food, a dog is taught to "sit"; later, when he wants a toy which he sees on a table, he goes to the table, assumes his "sitting" position, and barks?

Insights derive from an individual's best interpretations of what comes to him; they may be deeply discerning or they may be shallow. They may serve as dependable guides for action or they may prove ruinous. Chica, one of Köhler's apes, attempted to reach a banana by placing a box beneath it and jumping as high as possible from the box. After several failures, she suddenly held the box as high as possible, pressed it against the wall, and attempted to climb up on it. Chica had an insight, but not a true one.[7]

A person changes the cognitive structure of his life space through the *differentiation, generalization,* and *restructurization* of its respective regions. A region—a distinguishable, functional part of a life space—is the psychological meaning of an object or activity. The object or activity may be either a remembered, a contemplated, or a presently existing one. Regions of a life space may include conceptions of aspects of one's self, specific activities

[6] See Edward C. Tolman, "Cognitive Maps in Rats and Men," *Psychological Review*, July 1948, pp. 189–208.

[7] See Wolfgang Köhler, *The Mentality of Apes*, Vintage Books (New York: Random House, Inc., 1959), p. 139.

such as working and eating, states of being such as being frightened or feeling secure, and memberships in groups and classes as well as the personalities, objects, and events that one perceives. The cognitive structure of one's life space includes not only the arrangement and conditions of existing regions but also an understanding of what movements may occur and what may be the consequences of such movements. The relation of the region in which a person's activity is centered in reference to the other regions of his life delineates the qualities of his immediate surroundings, the kind of regions adjacent to other regions—possibilities for next steps, and what steps mean actions either toward or away from goals.

What is cognitive or perceptual differentiation?

Differentiation is the process within which regions are subdivided into smaller regions. In differentiation, relatively vague and unstructured regions of a life space become cognitively structured and more specific. Differentiation, then, means discerning more and more specific aspects of one's environment and oneself. What once were "kitties" come to be "leopards," "tigers," "lions," and "cats." What once was "bread" comes to be "crackers," "donuts," and "toast." What once was "baby" comes to be "me," "my arms," or "my legs," and, later, "student," "member of club," "ball player," and "lady-killer."

Differentiation proceeds at different rates at different times, and during crisis periods such as adolescence its speed rapidly fluctuates. As a child grows he differentiates (1) himself—his person—from his environment, (2) different aspects of his person and environment from each other, (3) a psychological past and future from the present, and (4) imaginative reality levels from the concrete reality level of his life space. Since the meanings of the latter two kinds of differentiation—differentiation of time perspective and differentiation of imaginative from concrete reality—are so often misunderstood, we explain them in some detail.

Differentiation in time perspective. During a person's development, an enlargement of his time perspective occurs; a psychological past and future become more significant. A small child lives very much in the present. His time perspective includes only an immediate past and an immediate future. However, as one's age increases, one's time perspective tends to expand. Thus, more and more remote future and past events influence present behavior. These time-binding events occupy such a central part of many adult life spaces that it is often assumed that a past and a future actually exist in their own right. Careful thought, however, will bring the realization that the only past with which a person can deal is *what he thinks happened in the past*. Likewise, the only future that can influence a person *now* is his *anticipation* of a future that he thinks may, or is going to, eventuate.

A child's present life situation contains traces, or "memories," of past incidents, but all of these are in his present situation or life space. When a second child has appeared in a family at some time in the past, the important factor now, as far as the first child is concerned, is not whether his mother rejected him when the second child was born, but whether he interpreted the past situation as one of rejection and carried the rejection into his present life space. The "past" can be of present significance only through operation of factors in the present which are identified as "past." That which persists from prior experience so that it is a "past" in the present is *trace*.

Anticipation of a future also occurs in the present; it is how one envisions the future, not what will actually happen then, that counts in the present. If a child is good in school on Monday so that he will get a star on Friday, whether or not he actually receives a star on Friday has nothing to do with his being good on Monday. His *anticipation* of the star is his motivation for his goodness on Monday. Recognition of the "presentness" of any past and future in no way depreciates them; it merely places them in a contemporaneous frame of reference within which growth of time perspective is in terms of memory traces and anticipations, which are functional parts of a present life space.

Differentiation of imaginative from concrete reality. Normal human development carries with it not only an enlargement of time perspecitve but also an increased differentiation of the concrete-imaginative dimensions of one's life space. As used in cognitive-field psychology, imaginative processes are wishing, dreaming, imagining, symbolic thinking, and kindred practices. To young children their products are concretely real; then gradually they are distinguished more and more from actual physical reality.

A young child does not clearly distinguish imaginary objects from concrete facts, wishes from goals, or hopes from expectations. Thus, to him, Santa Claus and Satan may be as real as any concrete object. However, when a child realizes that there "really" is no Santa Claus but still continues to talk about him, he is differentiating an imaginative realm from that of concrete reality.

Then, as he grows older, he tends to make an even sharper distinction between concrete and imaginative reality. True, fantasy in the form of wishful thinking is common in adults. However, they generally are better able to distinguish imaginative processes from concrete experience. Furthermore, mature adults should recognize the degree to which they are engaging in each.

How are concrete-imaginative levels related to time dimensions of a life space? The salient characteristics of a life space at any given juncture are (1) the level of concrete-imaginative reality at which the person is operating and (2) the degree to which the life space encompasses a psychological past and future. Furthermore, there is a direct relationship between the respective concrete-imaginative levels of reality and the degree of time-binding that pervades the life space of a person at a given time. At the level of concrete facts, immediate goals, and practical expectations, a life space contains only an incipient past and future; they are just beginning to be. Thus, concrete reality is to be found only in the momentary present. But, as a person's life space assumes more imaginative dimensions, his time-binding functions become increasingly extended and significant until, at an extremely imaginative level, his entire life space may be centered on either a psychological past or future. But, even then, the time and imaginative dimensions of a life space continue to be both contemporaneous and present.

We should not confuse the adjectives *imaginative* and *imaginary*; the two words have significantly different meanings. Whereas *imaginary* means purely fictitious or fanciful and existing only in the imagination, *imaginative* applies to that which arises through operation of one's imagination. Thus *imaginative* is a much more constructive term than is *imaginary*. In fact, a person's being imaginative is analogous to his being creative.

Imaginative levels of reality range from mere expectations and their means of fulfillment to hallucinations which give rise to extreme guilts and fears. Some levels between the two extremes, ranging from concrete reality to extremely imaginative reality, involve aspirations, wishes, imagination, symbolic thought, creativity, fancy, fantasy, dreams, and nightmares. In the psychological past, these take the form of memory, pride, innocence, error, fault, sin, and guilt. In the psychological future, they embrace goals, hopes, anticipations, conjectures, fabrications, visions, fears, and despair.

Figure 6 symbolically depicts the interrelationship of the concrete-imaginative dimension of a life space of a person and his

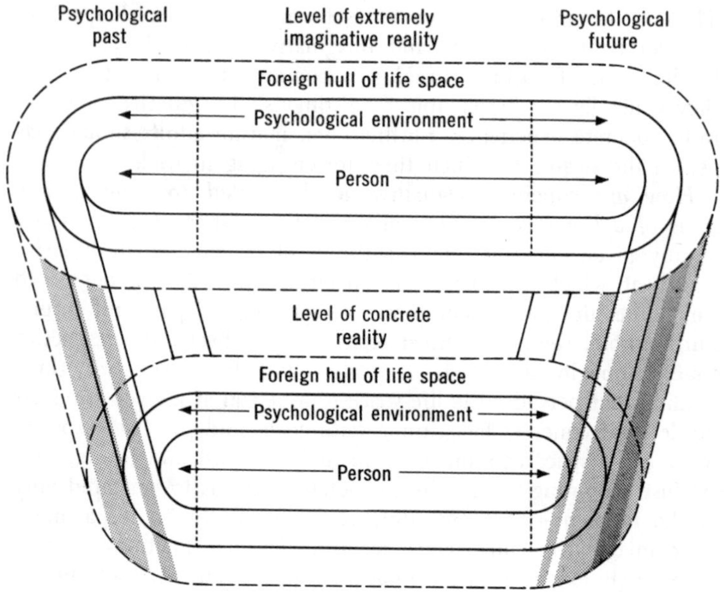

FIGURE 6. Concrete-imaginative levels of a life space as related to its psychological past and future.

time perspective. The figure should be interpreted to signify not merely two but several or even many levels of reality, which may range from life on a purely biological level to one of complete autism—absorption in fantasy. As a person functions on more imaginative levels, his psychological past and future also become more salient aspects of his life space. Thus, whereas on the level of concrete reality a psychological past and future hold only a relatively minor significance, as the person involved operates on more imaginative levels the time dimension of his life space becomes more and more important.

What is cognitive generalization?

Cognitive generalization is a process whereby one formulates a generic idea or concept through discernment of some common characteristics of a number of individual cases and identifies them as a class of ideas or objects. Thus, in cognitive-field terms, a generalization arises through a person's categorization of subregions into a unified region of his life space. When a child learns that vegetables, flowers, bushes, and trees are plants, or a student learns that his hopes, dreams, beliefs, and anticipations are all subregions of a "future" region in his contemporaneous life space, he is generalizing.

Although in common usage generalization is the opposite of differentiation, psychologically they are complementary. Generalization is the process whereby one groups a number of particular objects or functions under a single heading or in a single category. Thus, one generalizes when he forms a concept that includes previously differentiated aspects of himself or his environment. When a child learns that cats, dogs, horses, and birds are "animals" he is generalizing. Then, through a combination of differentiation and generalization, he may divide the physical world into vegetable, animal, and mineral.

What is cognitive restructurization?

Restructurization of one's life space means one's making more or different sense of oneself and one's world. A person not only differentiates and generalizes his life space into new regions but simultaneously restructures his life space; he changes the meanings of respective regions in relationship to himself and to one another. Within the process of restructurization, one defines or redefines directions in his life space; he learns what actions will lead to what results. He does this through perception of significant relationships of different functional regions of his life space. Restructurization, then, consists of separating certain regions that have been connected and connecting certain regions that have been separated. (Remember that regions are defined as functionally distinguishable parts of a life space.)

When we were quite young, most of us differentiated people from their environments. Later we differentiated people into various races, classes, and groups. Perhaps about the same time we generalized them into Republicans and Democrats, or Christians and non-Christians. As a person learns, he continues to differentiate and generalize himself and his environment, but he also restructures the differentiated and generalized regions of his life space so as to give them new meanings. In this way, a person becomes, or at least should become, an increasingly better thinker.

Restructurization includes, not only extensions of time perspectives and increased differentiation of imaginative from concrete levels of reality, but also changes in motivation and group identification and changes in bodily coordination. A person's change

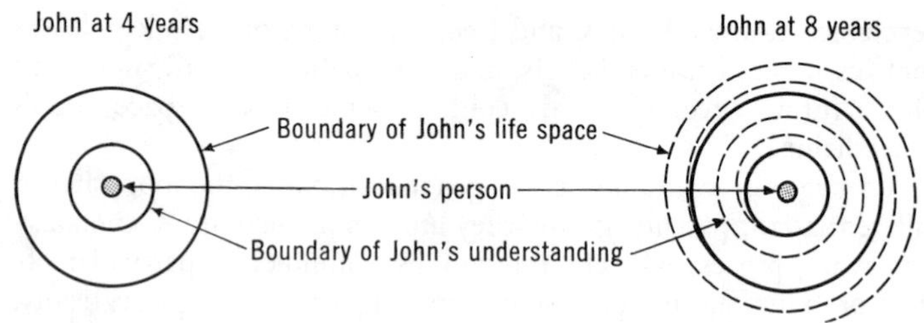

FIGURE 7. John's understanding of his life space at ages 4 and 8.

in motivation arises through his seeing regions or factors of his life space in a new light. To a 14-year-old boy, a girl, once something to be teased, comes to be a thing to be quite gently cuddled. A change in motivation is also closely related to changes in group identification. To a large degree it is the groups to which one belongs that are the source of his ideology and consequently of his motivation. One's person emerges through his becoming a member of a group and it develops as he changes his group allegiances. An adolescent's conformity to his peer group standards is a striking example of this developmental process.

A very noticeable evidence of a child's or youth's development is the change in control of his bodily muscular system—his bodily coordination. A small child gradually learns to handle himself quite well. Then comes the adolescent growth spurt. This entails such great changes in bodily size and proportions that a youth must almost start all over again in learning to control his musculature. This process ultimately becomes refined into development of the fine coordination of complex skills.

To a large degree a person's intelligence is dependent upon the degree of his change in motivation, bodily coordination, and time prespective, his differentiation of aspects of his person from those of his environment, and his discernment of levels of concrete and imaginative reality. As a child develops by means of these processes, he learns increasingly to understand and control his environment. However, teachers have no reason to fear that a student will soon acquire complete understanding and will see no further need to learn. The only person who may think he knows everything is the one who knows practically nothing. Once a student launches a serious study of his environment, his life space accelerates its rate of expansion. As his understanding expands to encompass newly gained regions of his life space, his life space also grows to such a degree that his motivation for study actually multiplies. This is illustrated graphically in Figure 7.

HOW IS OBSERVABLE BEHAVIOR CHANGE RELATED TO LEARNING?

Learning and change in observable behavior often occur side by side and seem to be interrelated. So, behaviorists contend that any change of behavior is learning, and conversely that any learning is a change of behavior. Thus, the current practice among many educators of defining learning as "change in behavior" usually reflects a behavioristic psychology.

For behaviorists, "*behavior*, as a technical psychological term, may be defined as the publicly observable activity of muscles or glands of external secretion as manifested for example in movements of parts of the body or the appearance of tears, sweat, saliva and so forth."[8] But, cognitive-field psychologists give *behavior* a quite different meaning. For them, it is any change in a person, his perceived environment, or the relation between the two that is subject to *psychological* principles or laws. *Psychological*, as used here, means involving purpose and intelligence.

Cognitive-field theorists think that logical empiricists and behaviorists err in making the observable results of learning synonymous with the learning itself. For them, a change of behavior may be evidence that learning has occurred or is occurring, but the behavioral change is not the learning. They contend that a change in physiological behavior does not necessarily mean that learning has occurred. A person who is in a dark alley and is struck from behind and knocked down may gain from this experience a healthy respect for dark alleys, but the change in behavior—falling down—is not equivalent to any change in insight that may have occurred. Furthermore, a person may use insights that he has gained through an earlier experience as the basis for a change in his present behavior. For example, an author may know that too much coffee is not good for him but persist in drinking coffee until he completes a manuscript, then reduce the amount of coffee he drinks. Probably many changes in the behavior of school children do not reflect their teachers' desired changes in student insights. Johnny may start saying "please" and "thank you" without an insightful

[8] D. O. Hebb, A *Textbook of Psychology*, 2nd ed. (Philadelphia: W. B. Saunders Company, 1966), p. 7.

grasp of the implications of his so doing, or he may labor hours every night over homework without having his work produce any change of mind about matters implicit in the homework itself.

Cognitive-field psychologists maintain that not only may a change in behavior occur without learning, but also learning may occur without any *observable*, related changes in behavior. This is true in innumerable situations. There may be an insight but no opportunity or occasion for a change in behavior, as when a person decides it would be nice to give more to charity but doesn't have the money to do so. Also, when new insights compete with older ones that have a strong hold on a person, the new insights may fail to change the person's behavior. For example, one may decide that racial discrimination is bad, but continue to practice it.

Because of their emphasis on behavioral change, many people with a behavioristic orientation think that doing something a number of times will necessarily affect one's future behavior. Thus, if one speaks a given word repeatedly for several days, its use will become habitual for one. Cognitive-field theorists deny that this is the case. Doing a thing either once or many times will affect subsequent behavior only to the degree in which doing it gives the doer a feeling for the act or insight into the consequences of its performance. It is the perceptual process, not the action as such, that is crucial. For this reason cognitive-field psychologists emphasize experience rather than behavior, with experience defined as an interactive event within which a person comes to see and feel the consequences of a given course of action, through acting and seeing what happens. When a person learns something, his behavior usually changes; but it does not follow that for learning to take place a change in observable behavior must occur at the same time, or that from a change in overt behavior we always can accurately infer the full nature of the insight related to it.

For positive relativists and cognitive-field psychologists, learning is a persistent change in knowledge, skills, attitudes, values, or beliefs. It may, or it may not, be reflected in changes in overt behavior. One does not "learn by doing" except insofar as one's doing contributes to a change in one's cognitive structure. For learning to result, doing must be accompanied by the doer's realization of the consequences of the act. Thus learning occurs through, and results from, experience; and "mere activity does not constitute experience."[9] For an activity to be included in experience,

[9] John Dewey, *Democracy and Education* (New York: The Macmillan Company, 1916), p. 163.

it must be interrelated with a realization of the consequences that accompany it.

HOW DOES LEARNING TRANSFER TO NEW SITUATIONS?

Transfer of learning occurs when a person's learning in one situation influences his learning and performance in other situations. If there were no transfer at all, students would need to be specifically taught every act that they were ever to perform in any situation. Although, when we think of transfer, we usually consider how one learning experience *strengthens* another, we should remember that there is also a negative transfer process within which one learning experience interferes with—*weakens*—another. However, generally speaking, what we learn in one situation tends to facilitate or help our learning in others. But the opposite effect, interference, can also occur. For example, a person's study of a foreign language or philosophy can make him a slower reader of English literature, or his becoming committed to certain dogmas or absolutes can interfere with his future creative, reflective thought.

The basic problem of transfer is: In what way and to what extent does the acquisition of skills, knowledge, understandings, and attitudes in one subject or learning situation influence performance or learning in other subjects or situations? Each educational philosophy has its respective theory of transfer and its own ideas in regard to how transfer is best promoted.

Logical empiricists assume that conditioning, either with or without reinforcement, of the behavior of organisms provides the basis for transfer. In keeping with their deterministic orientation, they think that any organism will respond according to its prior conditioning. So, whatever transfers to a new situation is all that could have done so.

Since idealists consider learning to be basically a process of mental unfoldment from within, they have relatively little interest in the phenomenon of transfer. Yet, their commitment to free will and kindred concepts leads them to embrace a self-initiated mental-discipline theory of transfer within which students discipline themselves through imitation of teachers and other mature persons.

Rational realists center their basis for transfer of learning in exercised mental faculties or a trained mind or intellect. They assume that once a mind is trained, its faculties automatically swing into operation when the occasion is appropriate for this to happen.

How does cognitive-field psychology treat transfer of learning?
For cognitive-field theorists, continuity of life spaces is the pivotal concept in their theory of transfer of learning. Along with perceptual interaction, which occurs in each life space of a person, there is a continuity of cognitive structures of succeeding life spaces. Although in the most technical sense a life space is of a moments' duration, for actual schoolroom purposes it is generally taken to extend over a juncture of some time. Furthermore, succeeding life spaces are not completely different from each other; rather, there is a continuity of a person's life spaces, and it is within this continuity that transfer of learning occurs. The cognitive structure of each life space overlaps, and shades into, that of the life which succeeds it.

Cognitive-field psychologists note that when transfer of learning occurs, it is in the form of generalizations, concepts, or insights that are developed in one learning situation being employed in others; this process is called *transposition*. Transposition of insights may also be described in terms of habits, but under cognitive-field psychology, habit has a special definition. A habit is a skillfully executed application of a principle in a situation wherein application of that principle will apparently help a person achieve a goal. Nevertheless, even habits are not blind, automatic behaviors. Rather, they are products of tested insights used in new situations. They are, therefore, precise adjustments to situations that call for them.

One may operate on habit, and transfer may occur with little or no reflection. Or transfer may occur in a highly reflective situation. In either case, transfer is not automatic. So habit is not an act that is repeated automatically simply because of its frequent repetition in the past. Neither is it a fixed sequence of acts that can be adequately explained as a system of preformed pathways in the nervous system. (Of course, some sort of concomitant neural action is not denied.) Habit, then, is fluid, effective, efficient action arising through a person's operating on the basis of the insights that he possesses. So, when one operates in terms of the insights or cognitive structure he has, habit is manifested.

Change in the cognitive structure of a life space through its differentiation, generalization, and restructurization means a change in meaning. Moreover, *a situation has meaning when it points to a course of action.* So, when an event has meaning, its psychological position and direction are determined; one knows what actions will lead to what results. This is the basis of habit. If a situation and its meaning are perceived simultaneously, then a person exhibits habit. Habit enables one to behave intelligently without thinking. Often there is not time to think; indeed, thinking then might be disastrous. What happens when your car is closely following a large truck and the truck stops abruptly?

How do cognitive-field psychologists promote transfer?

For learning to be most useful in future situations, it is essential that the insights gained should be generalized. But even then we cannot safely assert the transfer of the learned generalizations will occur automatically. Experience shows that in actual practice transfer of a generalization does not always occur even when a person understands a principle thoroughly and has applied it often. A natural scientist, for example, can be scientific in dealing with problems of natural science and at the same time resort to folklore and superstition in dealing with problems of the social sciences and humanities. He either may not recognize that scientific method is applicable to problems in the social sciences and humanities, or, recognizing it, have no desire to use it.

A person is in the best frame of mind for transfer to occur when he is aware of acquiring meanings and abilities that are widely applicable in learning and living. However, important as this is for cognitive-field psychologists, it is not enough. A person must also want to solve new problems or approach new situations in the light of the insights gained through previous experience. For transfer to occur, individuals must generalize—perceive common factors in different situations; they must comprehend them as applicable and appropriate to both, and thereby understand how the generalization can be used; and they must desire to benefit by the sensed commonality. Ernest E. Bayles tells us that any insight susceptible of generalized application "will transfer if and when—and only if and when—(1) opportunity offers, (2) a trained individual sees or senses it as an opoprtunity, and (3) he is disposed to take advantage of the opportunity."[10]

Cognitive-field theorists are committed to the proposition that

[10] *Democratic Educational Theory* (New York: Harper & Row, Publishers, 1960), p. 58.

transfer of learning to new tasks will be better if, in learning, the learner can discover relationships for himself, and if he has opportunities to apply his learning to a variety of tasks. Consequently, they think that, for transfer to occur at its highest level, we must help students understand many widely useful relationships, principles, or generalizations; we must foster sensitivity to the presence of opportunities for transfer so that likelihood of recognition is high; and we must encourage students to embrace goals, attitudes, and ideals which support the conviction that progressive refinement of outlook on life is possible and commendable.

What are some crucial points concerning transfer?
The crucial points of cognitive-field psychology in regard to transfer of learning and its promotion may be summarized in the following seven points:

1. Opportunity for transfer may occur in many situations. It is not inherent in any subject, but is possible from any field of knowledge.
2. Transfer is not dependent upon mental exercise with disciplinary school subjects.
3. Transfer is dependent upon methods of teaching and learning that use lifelike situations. It is facilitated by teaching for large generalizations that have transfer value.
4. Transfer is not automatic; opportunities for transfer must be recognized, and the person concerned must want to use them.
5. Transfer varies according to the difficulty of generalization of subject matter and the intellectual ability of individuals.
6. Insights need not be put into words for their transfer to occur.
7. The amount of intraproblem insightful learning, not the number of trials as such, determines the amount of interproblem transfer.

The subject matter of this chapter provides the psychological basis for, and leads into, Chapter 7, which describes the meaning of positive relativism for classroom practices, and Chapter 8, which explains how reflective teaching and learning proceed. But first we need to examine the nature of a democratic society and the implications of democracy for public education. This is treated in Chapter 6.

6

WHAT SHOULD BE THE ROLE OF SCHOOLS IN A DEMOCRATIC SOCIETY?

For schools to render the maximum service to society, it is essential that their structure and purposes should harmonize with the structure and purposes of that society. Accordingly, positive relativists think that a democratic society should be served by democratic schools. In this way, students would not only live democratically in school, but they would also learn what democratic living entails.

Positive relativists probably give democratic ideals and procedures a greater emphasis than do the adherents of any other philosophical position. They are convinced that democratic ideals should permeate not only the political structure of society but also all of its social institutions. The adherents of different educational philosophies generally recognize the etymological meaning of democracy as government by the people, but they vary greatly in their more specific understandings of the concept.

How do logical empiricists, idealists and rational realists characterize democracy?

Logical empiricists tend to think of democracy as a political system within which each mature and competent person, through voting, contributes his instructed judgment to a common good. They believe that people should make little or no attempt to arrive at consensus on decisional matters. Rather, each person should vote according to his own conscience, and majority rule should prevail. Since they emphasize the teaching of scientifically ascertained facts and reprove the indoctrination of values, logical-empiricistic schools and teachers, in instructing their students, strive to maintain complete neutrality in relation to social issues. They therefore promote axiological autonomy—freedom of students to arrive at their respective valuational positions all on their own. Consequently, within logical empiricism, democracy entails a school's compromise between factual indoctrination and valuational autonomy.

Idealists emphasize the *intrinsic* worth of each personality, and for them brotherhood is the essence of democracy. But they build their meaning of democracy upon fixed principles and inalienable rights. Hence democracy implies the inherent freedom of each person to express his intrinsic personality. Secondarily, idealists recognize the significance of each person as a member of society, but first and most important is his individualistic self-realization, self-expression, self-control, and self-direction. For idealists, democracy entails a spiritual unity within a social variety. Although people of all classes, races, and levels of ability are not to be welded into one piece, they are to be united in spirit and thereby in their efforts to pursue common ends. But all the while they are to preserve their distinctive qualities, which lend richness and variety to the whole populace.

For *rational realists* in education, democracy means that enlightened men generally search for the Common Good. It requires that people have both the ability to conduct such a search and the willingness to undertake and sustain it in all relevant situations. The Common Good consists in that which is good for all men, at all times, and in all places simply because they are men; it is discovered through enlightened inquiry into the absolutistic Nature of things. Accordingly, each individual's right to education should be limited only by his capacity to learn and society's ability to provide opportunities for him to do so. In this way, democracy entails a chance for each person to cultivate the classical ideal—to develop his aristocratic intellect as well as to prepare himself for practical matters.

Since educational philosophers interpret democracy in several different ways, positive relativists think it desirable to present their position in greater and more specific detail than is contained in the mere statement that they strive to promote democratic schools for a democratic society. They therefore develop their meaning of democracy as the prime characteristic of a unique kind of society, then determine what implications democracy, so construed, has for organized education.

How has the positive-relativistic meaning of democracy emerged? The two extreme, and basically absolutistic, forms of political organization are autocracy and anarchy. Within autocracy the people enjoy a high degree of *unequal freedom*. The leader—king, dictator, or teacher—exercises very great freedom at the expense of the freedoms of his subjects. Within anarchy, the ideal would be laissez faire—everyone would do as he pleased. Thus there would be *unlimited freedom* for all persons.

Early Western definitions of democracy often consisted in a compromise position that combined aspects of both autocracy and anarchy. Accordingly, democracy often was taken to be liberty or license for anyone to do as he pleased, provided the freedoms he enjoyed did not get in the way of his neighbors' also enjoying theirs. In this way democracy acquired a negative meaning. As a consequence, some autocratic individual or custom often was tolerated along with the negative "democracy" as an agent to enforce its freedoms. Quite often, in the performance of their judgmental function, leaders' exercise of absolute powers was accepted alongside permissive "democracy."

Positive relativists conceive modern functional democracy, not as a compromise, but as an emergent social structure that acquires its meaning through people's understanding of both autocracy and anarchy, their rising above them, and their formulating a new synthesis to replace the earlier compromise. The resulting conception of democracy is an emergent synthesis (see pages 2 and 14). Whereas autocracy implies unequal freedom and anarchy is characterized by unlimited freedom, democracy entails *equally limited freedom.* As a third-grader stated after his class had been discussing democratic ideas, "Then it is not what you will let me do or what I will let me do, but what we will let us do."

In our development of the proper role of democratic schools in a democratic society as viewed by positive relativists, we first examine some pertinent insights into, or characteristics of, any organized society. We then develop some of the more important relevant attributes of a democratic society. Next, we discuss how schools should interrelate with, and serve, such a society. Finally, and most important of all, we deal with the proper relationship of schools to their students. We will then be ready to consider what positive relativism implies for classroom practices; this is the subject of Chapter 7. Then the final chapter considers how reflective teaching and learning—the ideal of positive relativists—may be accomplished.

WHAT INSIGHTS CONCERNING ORGANIZED SOCIETY ARE PERTINENT TO THE ROLE OF ITS SCHOOLS?

The focal point of the cognitive-field psychology of positive relativism is experiences of individuals in relationship with other individuals and with groups. So, it is an interpersonal-social psychology. When we refer to it as interpersonal, we mean that the interrelationships of persons are very important. However, neither the development of persons nor the development of groups receives exclusive emphasis. Rather, the two processes are considered complementary. Just as groups cannot develop without persons, persons cannot develop independently of groups. Furthermore, the nature of persons is influenced greatly by the nature of the groups with which they identify. Likewise, the nature of groups is influenced by the nature of the interpersonal relationships within them.

Since a person's psychological environment is what he makes of his physical and social environments, the same supposed physical-social environmental unit provides different stimuli for different persons, and as the structures of successive life spaces of an individual change, they provide different stimuli for him. The state of an individual therefore includes not only his physical and biological condition but also his interpretive structurization of the supposed world as he experiences it. Such structurization is based partially upon the person's socialization as a member of society, and "the *social* perceptive system is primary, inclusive and determining of the geographical perceptual organization."[1] Our perception of the social, as well as of the physical, world is more a process of prognosis than one of disclosure. Its essence is predictive expectation, not proximate revelation.

A student in a class, like a person in a society, may be viewed simultaneously in two ways—both as a component part of a social unit and as a psychological person whose life space is structured within the limitations represented by the various social entities of which he is a part (see pages 21–22 for explanation of the concept *psychological person*). Professor Barker has reported:

> We found that we could predict some aspects of children's behavior more adequately from knowledge of the behavior characteristics of the drugstores, arithmetic classes, and basketball games they inhabited than from knowledge of the behavior tendencies of particular children.[2]

So, we recognize that the social environment of a community can, to some degree, coerce the behavior of the persons within it. Yet we also know that within limits each person, through his intelligent action in pursuance of his goals, can greatly influence the conditions of his life and activity. Thus, he can contribute markedly to his own destiny as well as to that of his society.

Although positive relativists constantly emphasize the importance of each person's goals, they simultaneously recognize that any idea of man's being separated from his interrelationship with, and dependence upon, his fellows or society is a self-deluding abstraction. Accordingly, the idea of absolute autonomy of individuals is a completely inadequate guideline for the direction of human affairs. The course of the cognitive structures of a person's life spaces, which are in continuous psychological movement, can be predicted accurately only within the ecological—physical-social—environments in which it proceeds.

For positive relativists, terms such as purpose, foresight, and

[1] *The Morning Notes of Adelbert Ames Jr.*, Hadley Cantril, ed. (New Brunswick, N.J.: Rutgers University Press, 1960), p. 186. (John Dewey writing to Ames).

[2] Roger G. Barker, *Ecological Psychology* (Stanford, Calif.: Stanford University Press, 1968), p. 4.

desire are scientific as well as literary expressions. But they in no way imply that the person is totally isolated in his individuality. A principal source or basis of each personality consists of the customs, beliefs, attitudes, values, and habits of the social groups within which an individual lives. What a person actually is in his life experience—his succession of life spaces—depends to a large extent upon the nature and purposes of his associated living.

Although a person does the best he knows how for whatever he thinks he is, through holding an inadequate conception of the person-social nature of human beings he may unwittingly injure himself. Overemphasis upon individualism can be pushed to the point where it actually discounts the dignity and worth of individuals; man is a cultural as well as a purposive and intelligent being.

WHAT ATTRIBUTES OF A DEMOCRATIC SOCIETY ARE RELEVANT TO ITS SCHOOLS?

A democracy, in its deeper sense, is a distinct mode of associated living. Its foundation is people's common confidence in their collective capacity to generate an adequate quality of knowledge within themselves for the effective guidance of their collective actions. Accordingly, both to promote the general welfare and to enhance the development of individuals, the persons who are involved must participate equally in formulating values and directing actions. Thus, in a democracy, people place their trust in themselves. They think that they collectively should have the ultimate right and power to determine, as far as humanly possible, the course of the affairs that influence their lives.

For positive relativists, democratic principles are nonabsolutistic ones. Whereas the existence of absolutes as such need not necessarily be either asserted or denied, democracy does imply that human beings should stand on their own feet, neither falling back on the strength of some absolutistic authority nor depending upon any absolutely fixed patterns of thinking for the solution of their problems. Instead, people should place their faith in the generalized intelligence of man, whom they consider to be immanently purposive in his pursuits.

Democracy, then, is the means whereby men of good will, despite their differences, continuously widen the area of their common interests. They root their morality in cooperative thinking and living and expand their cooperative outlook beyond a mere political arrangement to mutually established principles of living that apply to all phases of human activity. Consequently, the real problem of life within a democratic tradition is, How can each and all of us do the very best for each and all of us?

"A democratic social order which understands its own character and purpose to bound to have a distinctive system of education."[3] Hence, there should be a high degree of commonality between the basic philosophy and practices of schools in a democracy and the aspects of democracy that are most pertinent to education. Furthermore, the practice of democracy should not be confined to class, home room, and school council meetings, but should manifest itself in the basic functions of schools; namely, teaching and learning. It is therefore essential that all school personnel understand the structure and dynamics of the decision-making and decision-execution aspects of democracy; these are the characteristics most applicable to teaching-learning situations.

How is democracy a process of group decision making and enforcement?

Democracy has been defined by Professor Bayles as "*equality of opportunity to participate in making group decisions and equality of obligation to abide by them,* once they are made and until they are revised or rescinded."[4] In other words, democracy entails a social arrangement according to which all members of a group share equally in determining what freedoms and what restraints shall apply to all members of the group. In general, such freedoms are to be enjoyed, and restraints suffered, with equal force by all members of the group. The exception to this is that the group, in promotion of its own welfare and that of its members, creates certain offices and vests their holders with special powers for specific purposes; for example, police officers are vested with police powers.

In making group decisions, the ideal is consensus—a mutually agreeable position reached through discussion and concession and culminating in common consent. It is, however, often necessary for the group to act in the problem area being considered

[3] Boyd H. Bode, *Democracy as a Way of Life* (New York: The Macmillan Company, 1937), p. 62.

[4] Ernest E. Bayles, *Democratic Educational Theory* (New York: Harper & Row, Publishers, 1960), p. 157.

before a consensus can be reached. On such occasions a democratic group votes. Each person's vote is equal to that of anyone else, and a majority vote determines the basis for action. Note that votes are taken to facilitate actions, never to enforce common beliefs. Once a vote is taken, the losing minority as well as the winning majority must conform to its requirements. However, the minority need not change its thinking in regard to the issue; it doesn't have to like the decision. So, the rights of minorities, as well as those of the majority, are protected by freedom of speech or peaceable protest, freedom of thought, and prohibition of mob rule.

Certain other conditions contribute to the equitable and effectual functioning of democracy. If participation of members of a group is to be full and free, the group must develop an atmosphere of acceptance within which each member is considered important enough for his opinions to be heard and weighed. There should, therefore, be equality of opportunity for everyone to be informed, and all members of the group should be free to engage in mutual inquiry and persuasion.

A social or governmental unit need not have absolute power over its operations in order for democracy to prevail. Each group shares in the determination of policies of another group in the degree to which its interests are served by the activities of the second group; for example, states participate in setting policies for the cities within them, and decisions made by a city must conform to the laws set by the state of which it is a part.

What is the nature of democratic leadership?

A good democratic group leader should first of all serve as a unique type of inquiry and discussion leader. He may also act in an executive or administrative capacity, serve as an arbiter of issues within the group, and provide technical information to members. These latter functions are usually more prominent, but the real value of a leader depends upon his leadership in the solution of the group's problems.

A democratic leader of group inquiry leads the people in tackling significant issues, in defining the issues under study, and in clarifying the broader implications of the issues. Within the discussion process he asks related questions, listens to all members of his group, discovers and uses the potentials of all group members and resource persons, and points his group toward possible consensus. In this way he helps the group achieve significant self-growth. A group achieves self-growth through its members' (1) gaining better understanding of the group's function, (2) achieving fuller intercommunication, (3) developing shared responsibility in leadership and followership, (4) developing greater group cohesion, and (5) learning how to collect and use pertinent information, think straight, and make creative decisions in regard to problems. Now, what type of school-community relationship is conducive to a community's achievement of healthy self-growth? This is our next problem.

HOW SHOULD SCHOOLS SERVE A DEMOCRATIC SOCIETY?

A democratic society has a unique culture, and a basic problem of education involves the proper relationship of schools to that type of culture. *Culture* means the established way of life—the social heritage—of a people. It consists of all the socially transmitted results of human experience through which a group of people conducts its way of life. It includes customs, knowledge, morals, ideals, and standards and the institutions through which they are manifested.

Schools of today are expected to perform not only the functions of the schools of a century ago but also a multitude of other tasks deriving from the fact that much parental and community teaching which was once operative no longer functions. Not only are today's schools expected to teach many diverse matters (such as some vocational skills) which now are taught only by schools, they are also expected to help young people evaluate and make sense of the information and precepts presented by the mass media and other cultural agencies of instruction.

Controversy concerning the cultural role of schools centers on the extent of their obligation to their respective cultures. Obviously, schools are not the only agents that transmit culture and effect cultural changes. Homes, peer groups, churches, the mass media, and numerous other social organizations also participate in this function. Nevertheless, the task of schools in relation to their culture appears to be growing in importance. Yet there is much disagreement in regard to just how schools should serve the culture of which they are a part.

Most persons would agree that one of the chief functions of schools is to preserve, by transmitting to the young, that part of the culture regarded by most adults as good. However, performance of this task by itself makes education a highly conservative force. Schools that do no more than merely conserve a culture are appropriate to a static society, but not to one which is dynamic and rapidly changing. Hence, schools in a fast-moving culture should operate in relationship to change in such a way as to keep cultural innovations socially beneficial. Although citizen support for this twofold function of schools would probably be unanimous, it would be difficult to get agreement on just how the two tasks of cultural *conservation* and cultural *improvement* are to be performed simultaneously.

There are three basically different and conflicting attitudes in regard to a school's proper function in preserving and improving the culture. We may envision a school and likewise its staff, as performing the functions of (1) a cultural architect, (2) a conservator of the culture, or (3) a democratic leader in development of citizens' insights pertinent to amendment of the culture. To amend a culture is to modify it in some way for the better.

How do schools deem themselves architects of the culture?

Schools that perform the functions of a cultural architect provide the ideas and directives for renovating the culture in line with the thinking of the teachers and other educational experts in regard to what the culture *should be* like. Since schools systematically develop new cultural designs, this position is often identified as *social reconstructionism.* Obviously, it is an autocratic approach to education.

Teachers who adopt this position consider themselves expert innovators. In their thinking they design the specifications for an ideal culture just as an engineer designs a new machine. They then inculcate in students the knowledge, attitudes, and values that will cause new generations to move in the prescribed direction of this ideal. Since, to achieve their designed purpose, they indoctrinate and propagandize students, they are likely to promote ideas toward which considerable resistance will develop. However, since the teachers conceive themselves to be expert social engineers, they have little concern for the resistance they might engender.

How may school serve as conservators of the culture?

As conservators of the culture, schools serve their communities by perpetuating them in their existing forms. Thus, they preserve traditional knowledge, beliefs, attitudes, and values. To do this, they discover what now prevails and attempt to transmit it, intact, to a new generation. School leaders recognize that, like biological sports or mutations, cultural changes will be introduced through accidents of history and that often the changes which contribute to the welfare of the people will be perpetuated. But they think that schools should never deliberately become active agents of change. Moreover, they are likely to discourage unconventional thoughts in their students. In fact, teachers in conservative schools autocratically indoctrinate and propagandize their students much as do teachers who think that schools should function as social architects. However, the specific objectives of teachers in the two kinds of schools are quite different. Whereas conservative schools propagate the status quo, social-reconstruction-oriented ones deliberately lead students into predesigned social frontiers.

How do schools provide democratic leadership in development of insights pertinent to amendment of the culture?

Positive relativists think that schools should promote a study of the prevailing aspects of existing cultures, but always with the purpose of helping students develop insights pertinent to amending them—that is, changing them for the better. They think that the role of schools in a democracy is neither to change cultures in a striking and impetuous way nor to conserve them in their present forms. Instead, schools should help students to examine their cultures, to see the contradictions and confusions within them, and to find ways of progressively refining their own civilization as well as those of other societies.

When human nature is assumed to be neither bound to a natural-unfoldment process nor to be static, it encompasses all of the institutional achievements of a dynamic society. With sufficient application of human intelligence, a society can continue its growth in the direction of providing more adequate and harmonious living for all individuals involved. If schools are to aid substantially in such cultural progress, they must encourage students to study the culture of their own and other societies, but always with a view toward progressive refinement of those cultures.

When the subject matter under study is some aspect of the culture, the primary purpose of the investigation is neither to change it nor to preserve it, but to appraise it and strengthen its tenability through finding ways to improve it as it is being transmitted to new generations. Accordingly, an attempt is made to uncover contradictions and conflicts in a culture and to determine possible ways of resolving them, or at least preventing them from causing serious trouble. The ultimate hope of democratic schools is that the culture will be progressively refined by a citizenry that has learned the habit of studying problems in a reflective and democratic manner. So schools should foster social change, but help to keep it orderly and constructive.

A teacher, as a democratic leader in a democratic school, need not discard his personal preferences. Like either a social reconstructionist or a conservator of culture, he too holds certain ideas in preference to others. However, his method of teaching, unlike that of either a social reconstructionist or a conservator of culture, is the method of democracy. In a very real sense, he and his students, together, strive to gain more adequate insights for building a better culture. So, teachers must abandon traditional indoctrinative techniques of education and teach students how to discern, cooperatively with others, what a culture is and how it can be improved.

WHAT IS THE PROPER RELATIONSHIP OF SCHOOLS TO THEIR STUDENTS?

A school is a special environment created to facilitate learning; its principal business, therefore, is to enhance the learning process. For positive relativists, learning means the development of new insights or the changing of existing ones. Generalized insights become understandings. Understandings increase a person's intellectual capacity to make wise decisions. Accordingly, for both individuals and society, they are more valuable than isolated facts. In his endeavor to achieve insights there is no reason for a student to shun factual knowledge; nevertheless, generalized insights or understandings are what really count most.

Social and technological changes are now sweeping the world at such a rate that almost any specific fact or procedure taught today is likely to be obsolescent even before the learner leaves school. Consequently, a more serviceable goal for education than the mere accumulation of facts or behaviors is the creative discovery by the students of concepts and generalizations, and their development of thinking processes and cooperative learning skills. In this way, a student's achievement of significant school learning has much in common with a democratic society's resolving social issues. The achievement of learning in school is analogous to the process of making and executing decisions in politics.

Positive relativists recognize that democratic practices do prevail in some schools and to some degree. But they think that these practices and the outlook which supports them should be expanded to become the rule rather than the exception. Moreover, they have some ideas concerning how, in the long run, this can be achieved. They note that educational technology, like the industrial technologies, has tended to be forged within an autocratic framework. The primary reason for this is that both are patterned after a physicalistic, mechanistic conception of science as set over against a mentalistic, humanistic rationalism. However, democratic schools should not align themselves with either autocratic side of the issue; namely, either tough-minded, positivistic science or purely intellectualistic rationalism. Nor should they advocate some sort of autonomous anarchy. Instead, their role should be to frame an emergent from the three. The emergent would be a *humanistic, scientific, democratic outlook* and related procedures, promoted through reflective teaching, learning, and thinking.

In their thinking about the relationship of schools to students, positive relativists first observe that, even though the test-tube babies envisioned for the future would continue to be of the species *homo sapiens,* human evolution in its broader sense has not come to an end; man is still capable of fundamental developmental changes. The kind of hereditary influence that can continue to change the nature of man is social heredity of the products of human learning. Man collectively, through learning, can become a better kind of being than he now is or ever before has been.

Positive relativists recognize that we live in an industrial age when mechanistic training in the various technologies is greatly emphasized. They also note the fact that modern civilization has constantly been based upon some kind of interaction between technology and human values, and that for this interaction to develop we must refine the nature of the relationship. They further emphasize that a purely technological man is a myth; in evolution, previous existents do not completely die out. So man, to some degree and in some way, will continue to be humane.

Further reflections of positive relativists in regard to the proper relationship of schools to their students take somewhat the direction indicated in the following paragraphs.

Throughout the technological age, adults have guided the learning experiences of children and youth into two separate channels. One channel has been characterized by the autocratic imposition of pretechnological and technological factual matter the other, by the anarchistic permission of autonomously expressed unfoldment of supposedly innate features of the personality. However, when adults have been in the driver's seat, they have usually maintained a "safe" balance between large doses of autocratically imposed truths and small, respectable manifestations of the autonomous, individualistic expression of personality.

Current education, with its technological emphasis, tends to place both the objectives and the destiny of science ahead of those of human personalities, and many students now want this emphasis reversed. However, students often fail to see that human values must be developed reflectively along with technologies being discovered scientifically, and that reflective and scientific processes are very much alike. Reflective learning is man's careful, critical examination of a supposed article of knowledge in light of the testable evidence that supports it and the further conclusions toward which it points (see Chapter 7, pages 131–133 for expansion of this idea). Likewise, scientific procedure consists in the formulation and testing of hypotheses through empirical evidence gained by means of alert, unprejudiced, and controlled observation and experimentation.

Many critical students see modern technological education as well as conventional liberal education to be a fact-accumulation process, and tend to rebel against very much of it. These students are willing to spend a small percentage of their time absorbing facts, but they want these facts to be immediately relevant to life and a vocation. They then want to devote the remaining, larger segment of their school time to self-expression, self-actualization, and self-realization, guided only by their inner feelings and choices.

Being very poorly oriented in regard to the basic nature of a democratic social structure and educational institutions, these students merely desire to shift the educational balance from one end of the beam to the other. They do not necessarily desire to change the basic nature of the two weights; namely, autocracy and autonomy. As the students see their current educational world, they are pushing for a heart-centered education as contrasted with either a mind- or an eye-centered one—for an education based on feelings rather than on either rationality or empirical science.

In political terms, our traditional schools, in dealing with students, have most often been about nine-tenths autocratic and one-tenth anarchic. Student leaders now often seem to desire a shift in the learning atmosphere to one that is about nine-tenths anarchic and one-tenth autocratic, but neither balance adequately serves the needs of our present and future democratic society. We do not achieve a viable democracy through a compromise between autocracy and anarchy, or in fact a *compromise* between any other forms of organization. It is quite true that within a democracy, when people must act and a consensus is not possible, they resort to compromise. Nevertheless, an effectual democracy cannot be built on a compromise in its basic social theory.

Most learners sincerely want to change things for the better, but many, because of improper earlier learning experiences, have not learned how to build a better world through cooperative inquiry and dissent. In teaching their children and youth, adults have too often failed to instill the idea of the necessity for built-in change to characterize democratic institutions and society. Many learners honestly feel that, even in a democratic society, the only real tools for progress are either destructive violence or "far out" group-therapeutic experiences. However, genuine change built into the methods and results of democratic teaching and administration would preclude a need for revolutions.

Boyd H. Bode's statement in 1947 anticipated the basic dilemma of today's schools. He wrote, "The most serious indictment that can be brought against our present-day system of public education is that it leaves our young people without a definite sense of direction."[5] So, we must have the deliberate aim of helping learners of all ages to develop a viable democratic personal-social outlook and a set of technological vocational skills as well, and these two sets of purposes need not be isolated from one another.

Now, let us consider some of the more obvious characteristics and consequences of autocratic, anarchic, and democratic teaching situations and procedures as they relate to students. Advocates of all three positions desire to liberate human intelligence from the evils of war, poverty, racism, ignorance, and disease. In a positive vein, all three want a peaceful, productive society. But there is a great divergence in the ideas of adherents of the three positions in regard to how these goals best may be attained. To sharpen the issue: Is man a passive, complex machine? Is he a

[5] Boyd H. Bode, et al., *Modern Education and Human Values* (Pittsburgh, Pa.: University of Pittsburgh Press, 1947), p. 15.

subjectively free, autonomously flowering self? Or is he a purposive person who develops through his interaction with his socio-psychological environment? To repeat once again, interaction, as used here, means a person's, psychologically, simultaneously reaching out to his environment, acting in relation to it, and realizing the consequences of his action. In other words, it is a process whereby a self, or person, as a center of values and insights uses his psychological environment in the development and achievement of his purposes.

How do authoritarian schools relate to students?

In authoritarian schools teachers exercise firm, centralized control. They closely direct the actions of their students. They do all the planning for the classes and issue all the directions. Furthermore, they tell students what to think as well as what to do. In an authoritarian classroom, a teacher regards himself as the sole active agent and considers students passive receivers of instructions and information.

The most efficient modern version of autocratic teaching is probably that based on the deterministic *operant conditioning* theory of B. F. Skinner of Harvard. Professor Skinner's psychology is strictly an engineering type of science. He insists that psychology is a science of preponderantly overt behavior. Accordingly, he defines learning as a change in the probability of responses. In most cases this change is brought about by operant conditioning—the learning process whereby a response is made more probable or more frequent; an operant is strengthened, that is, reinforced. An operant is a set of acts that constitutes an organism's doing something—raising its head, pushing a lever, or saying "horse." Through operant reinforcement we supposedly learn to keep our balance, talk, walk, play games, handle tools, paint pictures, master English grammar, and think about mathematics.

Skinner's basic thesis is that since an organism, including man, tends to do in the future what it was doing at the time of reinforcement, one can, by baiting each step of the way, lead the organism to do very much what the experimenter or teacher wishes it to do. Using this thesis as a basis for his procedure, he has taught rats to use a marble to obtain food from a vending machine, pigeons to play a modified game of tennis, dogs to operate the pedal of a refuse can to retrieve a bone, and psychotic patients to behave in a more desirable manner.

Skinner is convinced that operant conditioning, so fruitful when applied to animal training, promises equal success when used in schools. He recognizes the first task of teachers to be to shape proper responses; for example, to get children to pronounce and write responses properly. But he sees their principal task as bringing proper behavior under many sorts of stimulus control. Accordingly, he writes, "Teaching spelling is mainly a process of shaping complex forms of behavior. In other subjects—for example, arithmetic—responses must be brought under control of appropriate stimuli."[6] To achieve this task, Skinner recommends the use of programmed instruction. This may be accomplished either with or without the use of teaching machines. (See Chapter 7, page 117 for further treatment of operant conditioning.)

How would laissez-faire schools relate to students?

In laissez-faire schools, teachers and other professional personnel would not really lead the students in any manner. Teachers would be present, they might answer questions, but essentially students would be permitted to follow their own initiative. The students would decide what they would do and when they would do it.

The laissez-faire or autonomic goal of teaching has been ably presented by Professor Jurgen Herbst of the University of Wisconsin. Herbst feels that life is too rich to be captured in subject matter and that the content of any curriculum is too limited to represent the reason for the existence of schools. For him, the objective of teaching is neither transmission of factual information, promotion of socialization, nor indoctrination in scientific methods and technologies, but the achievement of personal autonomy. Accordingly, mere experiencing and reasoning processes should give way to a learning that is both spontaneous and purposeful.

Hence, the function and task of schools should be to provide conditions under which personal autonomy may emerge and be sustained, protected, and nurtured. And to quote Herbst, "Autonomy does not mean the principled rejection of authority but rather the ability to accept or reject it in the light of your own consistent standards."[7] Since teaching means to free people from their dependence on others, to stand them on their own feet and

[6] B. F. Skinner, *Cumulative Record* (New York: Appleton-Century-Crofts, 1959), p. 165.

[7] Jurgen Herbst, "The Anti-School—Some Reflections on Teaching," *Educational Theory*, vol. 18, no. 1 (Winter 1968), p. 22.

encourage them to walk for themselves, it must be free of all social and conceptual restraints. The aim of learning is the fullest understanding of man's experience of the world, and mastery of it consists in ordering experience through structures and interpretations created by the students themselves.

Although the idea of students' autonomous expression of their independent selves is presently being promoted quite widely, especially by philosophical existentialists, a human person apart from a society is for positive relativists either a myth or a monstrosity. The use of democratic processes therefore becomes a superior alternative to teachers' treating fellow learners either as complex machines or as subjectively free, autonomous beings.

How do democratic schools relate to students?

In its deeper meaning, democratic education is a process of helping students in the formation of fundamental intellectual-emotional dispositions toward the world, including their fellow men. In other words, education "is that reconstruction or reorganization of experience which adds to the meaning of experience, and which increases ability to direct the course of subsequent experience."[8] Teaching should be pointed toward experiences that assist students in making their outlooks more adequate and more harmonious and thereby more serviceable as guides for actions. Accordingly, it should be more exploratory than explanatory and more provocative than evocative. That is, it should teach people how to think more than what to think. Thus, it should strive to produce partisans, but be nonpartisan in the achievement of this task.

In a democratic teaching-learning situation the teacher plays the role of a democratic group leader. His chief purpose is to lead his students in the study of significant problems in the knowledge area in which he is teaching. Such study presupposes interchange of evidence and insights, give-and-take, and respect for one another's ideas. In a democratic classroom, the teacher's ideas are subject to both students' and the teacher's vigorous criticism just as are those of students. In this way both students and teacher learn; they reconstruct their life spaces so as to give them more meaning. Although a teacher may be an authority on his subject —and to teach it best he should be—the school situation is so arranged that students are encouraged to think for themselves

[8] John Dewey, *Democracy and Education* (New York: The Macmillan Company, 1916), p. 89.

in the interest of their long-sighted well-being. To *think* means to arrive at an effective conclusion based upon a substantial amount of checkable empirical evidence.

There are cogent reasons why consistently democratic school relations should be substituted for autocratic and anarchic ones. It ill behooves a nation that is straining in democratic directions to maintain in its schoolrooms nondemocratic relationships between teachers and students. Furthermore, evidence now available suggests that students probably learn more effectively in a democratic than in either an authoritarian or a highly permissive classroom.[9]

Positive relativists realize that, in recent years and in many places, the idea of democratic schools has fallen into ill repute. They see two basic, but unfortunate, reasons for this. The first reason is that wooly-minded individuals often have mistaken anarchic situations for democratic ones. But positive relativists contend that truly democratic teachers hold no brief whatsoever for laissez-faire classrooms. Indeed it is tragic for educators to call any uncontrolled and undirected classrooms "democratic." The second reason for the ill repute of democratic schools is that meanings of the terms *democratic* and *democracy* have often become perverted; as applied to teaching they have come to mean "easy," "soft," or "undisciplined." However, a democratic group may in fact work at the maximum level that health permits, and its manner of operation may be fully as rigorous as that of any scientific investigation. Furthermore, "basing education upon [students'] personal experience may mean more multiplied and more intimate contacts between the mature and the immature than ever existed in the traditional school, and consequently more, rather than less, guidance by others."[10]

In their commitment to democratic education, positive relativists do not attempt to make education exclusively scientific in the same conventional manner as do logical empiricists. However, they do promote creative thinking in every way possible, and this is the heart and spirit of twentieth-century science. Thus, they emphasize employment of relativistic scientific procedures. For them, "progress [in science] means increase of present meaning, which involves multiplication of sensed distinctions as well as

[9] See Bayles, *Democratic Educational Theory,* chap. 1, "Experments with Reflective Teaching."

[10] John Dewey, *Experience and Education* (New York: The Macmillan Company, 1938), p. 8.

harmony, unification."[11] Such progress is achieved through employment of serviceable models or paradigms to implement their thinking. A paradigm is a generally recognized scientific achievement that for a time provides model problems and types of solutions for a community of scientific practitioners.[12] The basic scientific paradigm of positive relativism is immanently purposive men cooperatively making sense of themselves and their environments in such a way as to do the most possible for themselves.

Civilization grows through a process of man's carefully casting and testing hypotheses through his imaginative use of abstractions. Without abstractions there is no scientific method, and abstractions, of necessity, extend beyond practical—immediate—matters. So, for scientific inquiry to occur in any field, the persons participating in it must remove their thinking, at least temporarily, from entanglements with immediate needs. Nevertheless, in scientific pursuits, men do pursue the goals of long-sighted self-interests. What counts most is the foreseeable consequences of proposed lines of conduct in terms of their bearing upon human life and relationships.

Teachers must be both equipped and disposed to serve as active chairmen of investigational bodies—to teach reflectively. Reflective teaching is teacher-student cooperative, exploratory teaching, which involves both problem development and problem solution. It is based on the conviction that a student studies and learns best when he seeks the relevance of his learning to what he intelligently needs. A problem is a psychological phenomenon that involves psychological tensions in a learner. Thus, it is immanent, not transcendental, to the stream of experience.

In the process of reflective teaching, teachers constantly persuade and induce students to reconstruct, reorganize, and reinterpret their own experiences. When reflective teaching is successful, students become perplexed just short of frustration, and they emerge with an enlarged store of generalized insights and an enhanced ability and desire to develop and solve problems on their own.

[11] John Dewey, *Human Nature and Conduct* (New York: Holt, Rinehart and Winston, Inc., 1922), p. 283.

[12] See Thomas S. Kuhn, *The Structure of Scientific Revolutions*, in *International Encyclopedia of Unified Science*, vol. 11, no. 2 (Chicago: The University of Chicago Press, 1962), chaps. 1–3.

7

WHAT DOES A POSITIVE-RELATIVISTIC EDUCATIONAL PHILOSOPHY MEAN FOR CLASSROOM PRACTICES?

The primary goal of teaching is the enhancement of learning. So, when educational philosophers concern themselves with teaching as such, they develop what they think are the best procedures for promotion of highly effectual learning. But the adherents of each philosophy have their own unique approach to the nature and enhancement of the teaching-learning process.

Conventional teaching procedures and classroom practices were devised at an earlier time, when the principal task of teachers was to communicate the proper information to students and the desired outcome of teaching was simply the students' memorization of that information. Even now, students' desire to *explore* knowledge is often submerged in their being *compelled* to acquire it. Consequently, "learning tends to get increasingly lost behind externalized acquisition of data."[1] In various degrees, adherents of the respective contemporary educational philosophies are attempting to provide intellectual leadership for the improvement of teaching. But the techniques recommended for achievement of the desired changes vary greatly from philosophy to philosophy.

WHAT ARE THE PURPOSE AND NATURE OF TEACHING?

Logical empiricists, idealists, rational realists, and positive relativists have their respective ideas regarding what teachers should be doing and how they should be doing it. The positive-relativistic approach to teaching-learning is given clearer definition when it is contrasted with the positions represented by other educational philosophies. In this section of the chapter, therefore, we briefly explore how logical empiricists, idealists, and rational realists each characterize the teaching process. Then, in more detail, we explain the position of positive relativists. In the following section, we develop the various levels of teaching-learning and relate them to the respective philosophies. Next, we briefly describe reflective teaching-learning—the positive-relativistic ideal. In the final section, we relate methods of evaluation to different teaching-learning levels, and explore how a positive-relativistic approach to evaluation differs from the approaches of other philosophic positions. Then, in Chapter 8, we discuss how reflective teaching and learning proceed.

How do logical empiricists view the purpose and nature of teaching?

Logical empiricists embrace a naturalistic, deterministic view of human beings, one which considers their drives and interests, their reflections and deliberations, their purposes and ideals, and their choices and actions, all "as links in the causal chains of the

[1] Rollo May, *Psychology and the Human Dilemma* (New York: Van Nostrand Reinhold Company, 1967), p. 45.

processes of the universe."[2] Within this philosophic position, "only the deterministic view provides an adequate basis for an interpretation of moral responsibility."[3]

Since logical empiricists interpret all learning in terms of caused changes in observable behavior, they consider teaching to be the process of causing the desired behavioral changes in students. Accordingly, teachers or other school authorities decide which specific responses they want students to display. They then stimulate the student in such a way as to evoke and reinforce the desired behavioral responses. The success of the process is judged by how dependably the behavior is manifested in the future.

For logical empiricists, teaching is a process of conditioning passive biological organisms. Conditioning is any sort of stimulus-and-response manipulation that results in either an enduring change in the behavior of a given organism or an increase in the likelihood of occurrence of a certain behavior. Conditioning takes the form either of stimulus substitution or response modification. Stimulus substitution is called classical conditioning; it is based on an adhesive or associative principle. (This is what Pavlov used on his dog.) Response modification is called instrumental or operant conditioning; it is based on a feedback or reinforcement principle.

Probably the most efficient mechanistic method of changing the behavior of either students or rats involves the use of programmed instruction, or in other words operant conditioning. Programmed instruction is a system of teaching and learning within which preestablished subject matter is broken down into small, discrete steps and carefully organized into a logical sequence in which it can be learned readily by the students. Each step builds deliberately upon the preceding one. The learner can progress through the sequence of steps at his own rate, and he is reinforced immediately after each step. In a rat or a very young child, reinforcement consists in receiving small parcels of food or other organically satisfying substances. In an older child, or an adult, it consists in his being either given the correct answer or permitted to proceed to the next step immediately after he has registered the correct response.

Positive relativists and other critics of programming often observe

[2] Herbert Feigl, "Aims of Education for Our Age of Science: Reflections of a Logical Empiricist," in Nelson B. Henry, ed., *Modern Philosophies and Education* (Chicago: The University of Chicago Press, 1955), p. 322.

[3] *Ibid.*, p. 322.

that a system of programmed instruction, when left to itself, as it is when administered by a teaching machine, tends to make students behave in a mechanistic fashion. Thus, it places a "machine" at each end of the handle. To quote Rollo May:

> We then tend more and more to ask only questions the machine can answer, we teach more and more only the things the machine can teach, and limit our research to the quantitative work the machines can do. There is bound to emerge a real and inexorable tendency to make our image of man over into the image of the very machine by which we study and control him.[4]

For idealism, what is teaching?

Within idealism, the primary purpose of teaching is to foster the active self-realization or self-perfection of each student, who is regarded as a spiritual being. The self-realization or -perfection is derived from a connection with and belief in a Universal Self. Thus, "all education, within idealist intentions, deals in the end with matters of faith, not only with morals."[5]

Teaching, first of all, consists in the teacher's setting a proper example for students to imitate—that of an active, mature person living in a creative fashion. The teacher creates his students' educational environment and provides their chief source of inspiration. Accordingly, he constantly inspires those purposive, active responses of learners that are promoted by the learners' inherent interest in their work. Within the teaching-learning process, solid book learning and lecturing are tempered by some slight feeling of suspense in students that is promoted through teacher-led questioning and discussion. "Since it is the self-activity of the pupil in which genuine education and development take place, he [an idealist] wants the student to be confronted by decision and selection as much of the time as possible."[6] Students live their way into a system of thinking, rather than think their way into a system of living.

How do rational realists view the purpose and nature of teaching?

For rational realists, "education is the art of communicating truth."[7] Truth may be gained in regard to both incidental matters

[4] *Op. cit.*, p. 173.

[5] J. Donald Butler, *Idealism in Education* (New York: Harper & Row, Publishers, 1966), p. 131.

[6] *Ibid.*, pp. 117–118.

[7] John Wild, "Education and Human Society: A Realistic View," in Nelson B. Henry, ed., *Modern Philosophies and Education* (Chicago: The University of Chicago Press, 1955), p. 31.

and essential forms. However, "the forms of things are their most important parts."[8] Whereas formal knowledge is theoretical, incidental education is vocationally oriented. The way to teach students things is to help them apprehend their *real* forms, which are in the things themselves. Through "general education," the most important kind, teachers should promote knowledge of classical models of excellence—those forever relevant.

For rational realists, education is intellectual; it emphasizes symbols, language, and theory. Rational realists, like idealists, emphasize students' achievement of freedom, self-actualization, and integration. However, they stress the intellectual (as opposed to the idealists' emphasis of the emotional) nature of this process. Students' intellects must be developed to the point that, to some degree, they can gain the Truth as it really is.

Although rational realists' ideas are anchored in antiquity, they seem to represent a compromise position between idealism, which also goes back to the ancients, and logical empiricism, which has emerged in the present century. This compromise is evidenced most clearly by rational realists' tendency to dichotomize—split in two—many mutually complementary concepts into antinomies. Some examples of such dichotomies are form vs. matter, mind vs. body, intellectual or liberal vs. vocational, and theory vs. practice. So, in their approach to teaching, rational realists seem to draw upon both idealistic and logical-empiricistic principles. Their primary emphasis on forms, minds, intellects, and theory seems idealistic; but their recognition of a secondary level of reality, which involves matter, bodies, vocations, and practice, reminds one of the position of logical empiricists.

How does positive relativism treat the purpose and nature of teaching?

For positive relativists, learning involves persons' purposive development of more adequate individual insights or understandings; their extension of knowledge and discovery; their fashioning of artistic creations; their promotion of ties that hold them together in mutual aid and affection; and their expansion of areas of common goals and purposes through the harmonization of their thoughts and interests. Through learning so conceived, knowledge becomes a power that may be used experimentally for the benefit of individual selves and all mankind. Thus, through the development

[8] Harry S. Broudy, "A Classical Realist View of Education," in Philip H. Phenix, ed., *Philosophies of Education* (New York: John Wiley & Sons, Inc., 1961), p. 19.

and use of knowledge, man can change himself, transform his habits, broaden his life activity, and give his perspective a wider scope.

The key to improvement of present and future learning is the reconstruction of teaching-learning processes and materials so as to prepare people for today's (and, to the best of our ability, tomorrow's) vocational and cultural world. But this should be accomplished in such way as to enhance both the intellectual and moral values germane to each life and vocation. Hence, all learning that is socially necessary should receive humane direction. But in contrast to the approach of rational realism, there should be no sharp distinction between liberal and vocational studies.

Since positive relativists are convinced that any person does the best he knows how for whatever he thinks he is, they adhere to some form of cognitive-field psychology, which emphasizes the immanent purposiveness of human beings. Accordingly, they think that the tension that motivates a person to learn is tension *toward a goal.* Whereas logical-empiricistic behaviorism is a mechanistic, deterministic—basically nonpurposive—psychology, cognitive-field psychology centers upon man's apparent immanent purposiveness. Whereas behaviorists interpret learning in terms of changes in strength of hypothetical variables called S-R connections, associations, habit strengths, or behavioral tendencies, cognitive-field theorists define it in terms of reorganization of perceptual or cognitive fields or systems. Consequently, whereas a behavioristic teacher desires to change the behaviors of his students significantly in a specified way, a cognitive-field-oriented teacher aspires to help students change their understandings of significant problems and situations, and he leaves it to students to develop their own behaviors based upon their enhanced understanding of themselves and the world about them and of their behavioral potentials in relation to this world.

To summarize the positive-relativistic cognitive-field theory of learning as presented in Chapter 5, we may say that a person learns through differentiating, generalizing, and restructuring his person and his psychological environment in such way as to acquire new or changed insights, understandings, discernments, or meanings concerning them, and thereby achieves changes in motivation, group belongingness, time perspective, and ideology. In this way, he gains greater control of himself and his world. So learning, concisely defined, is a process of persons' gaining or changing their insights, outlooks, or thought patterns.

Cognitive-field theorists, in thinking about the learning processes of students, prefer the terms *person* to *organism, psychological environment* to *physical* or *biological environment,* and *interaction* to either *action* or *reaction.* Such preference is not merely a whim; there is a conviction that the concepts *person, psychological environment,* and *interaction* are highly advantageous for teachers in describing learning processes. They enable a teacher to see a person, his environment, and his interaction with his environment all occurring at once; this is the meaning of "field."

Teaching, then, should be identified with teacher-student research in the area concerned. What is learned is not a set of behaviors as such, but rather both one's own behavioral potentials and the behavior that may be *expected* from other things or persons. Hence learning is connecting related things or ideas and inserting them into structures that give them significance. In so doing, a learner gains insights, understandings, or generalizations. Each area of knowledge, then, consists of a structure of interrelated concepts along with some conceptual models that give meaning to the facts that are involved and thereby make possible the deduction of new facts and generalizations.

A teacher who accepts the cognitive-field conception of man approaches human motivation in a fundamentally different way from one who operates within a behavioristic framework. He is always concerned with the involvement of his students in real problems—situations that involve personal tensions. In this way he helps them see a need to learn. However, he does not cater to every student whim. Rather, he constantly prompts students to rethink their goals and discard those that are merely trivial or whimsical.

A goal may be either positive or negative—something one wants to achieve or something one wants to avoid. When a barrier—any obstacle to the direct and immediate achievement of a goal—appears, a person feels tension. He tries to relieve tension by either surmounting or circumventing the barrier. His motivation is his tendency either to relieve or to equate tensions by proceeding toward a positive or away from a negative goal, and overcoming whatever barriers are in the way. The particular form that motivation takes, and its intensity, are functions of the field of psychological forces within which no distinction can be made between "inner" and "outer." That is, one cannot identify a category of forces that stem exclusively from physiological drives and another category that stem from the outside environment.

Emotion or affect, then, is a byproduct of the way people apply themselves to life situations, not something they should strive for as such.

Since a life space, strictly speaking, is a momentary situation involving a specific person and his specific psychological environment, one's experience consists of a series of overlapping momentary life spaces, each to some degree different from the one that preceded it. Thus, within the stream of one's experience, one's psychological environment as well as one's person is constantly changing. Furthermore, what *appears* to *an observer* to constitute the environment of a student (let us call him George) may include many elements not actually in George's psychological environment, and the observed environment may exclude some elements that, for George, psychologically are in it. To understand George, the teacher must study George in George's psychological environment, not merely the physical-social environment.

Thus, to be objective in dealing with a student, a teacher must also be subjective. George's teacher must see the world as George sees it. In order to predict George's behavior accurately, he must understand the interactive nature of regions of George's life space —his person and his environment—and he must be able to predict (anticipate) the boy's future life spaces. Then, for the teacher to be able to teach George in a significant manner, it is imperative that there be some intersection of regions of George's life space with those of the teacher and with regions of the life spaces of the other students in the room.

All this means that, to deal with a student most effectively, a teacher must think, "If I were this student's age and had his psychological environment and a system of insights and values similar to his, what would I be trying to do and why would I be trying to do it?" A teacher's unique function is to implement the development of serviceable insights of students so as to help them become more adequate and harmonious personalities—i.e., to become more intelligent.

If he is to teach other persons in a significant way, a teacher should have sympathetic understanding of students as persons and should strive to develop an accurate idea of what is actually transpiring in the life spaces of those whom he is teaching. To gain an understanding of each person and his cognitive world, a teacher needs to develop a sort of disciplined naiveté; he must see the student's person and environment as the student sees them. In order to succeed in seeing a student through, *he must see through him.* In other words, a teacher should strive to construe his students' "construings."

A teacher should have an extensive background of varied knowledge; he should be alert to the attitudes and outlooks that students are developing; and his ideal should be to promote an atmosphere that fosters maximum insightful growth. This means that he should be able to judge which attitudes or insights are conducive, and which are detrimental, to continued growth.

Advocates of cognitive-field psychology think that a teacher should teach; neither baby-sit nor dictate. A baby-sitter usually performs a custodial function but teaches children little. A dictator imposes the "right" answers. A teacher, in contrast with both, should perform his democratic teaching role in a process of student-teacher mutual inquiry. Teaching for insight or understanding can be either reflective or nonreflective, but democratic teaching should always strive toward reflective procedures (reflective teaching is described on pages 158–172).

WHAT LEVELS OF TEACHING-LEARNING SHOULD BE PURSUED?

Based upon the degree of thoughtfulness that is involved, teaching-learning situations may be categorized into four levels—*memory, autonomous development, understanding,* and *reflection.* Understandings, insights, or discernments are desired products of both the understanding and the reflection levels. But, the goals of reflection-level teaching-learning are *purposively acquired* understandings, insights, or discernments *plus* the learners' increased abilities to achieve further understandings, insights, or discernments through the use of a scientific outlook and instrumental thinking.

Positive relativists think that all teaching should be pointed toward either the understanding or the reflection level, and that, as much as possible, it should be held on the reflection level. They recognize that there are few, if any, teachers who can hold teaching and learning on a reflection level all the time. Thus, teaching that is focused on a reflection level will slip into the understanding level part of the time. But it seldom, if ever, will be based on a pure memory level per se.

Positive relativists certainly do not object to having students learn facts and remember them for future use. However, facts with no theory or rules to unify them tell one little of what to expect in new situations. Consequently, they equip people to operate only in routine situations where the specific answers have already been acquired. The emphasis of positive relativists is therefore upon students' growing to see the world and themselves differently, thereby enhancing the quality of their expectations, and it is within this process that facts are acquired and used.

Accordingly, adherents of positive relativism emphasize that facts are learned best when they are regarded by learners as instruments for serving purposes that they feel are important—when they are connected with problem solving. To positive relativists, a background of factual information or skills, unless it has sufficient bearing on the common problems of life to furnish hypotheses and data pertinent to their verification, is rather useless. Consequently, an educational program consistent with a positive-relativistic educational philosophy focuses on teaching students to think more effectively in a wide variety of situations; it entails problem-centered reflective teaching.

What about memory-level learning and teaching?

Memory-level learning is the kind of learning that supposedly involves students' committing factual materials to memory and nothing else. We all know that it is possible for a person to memorize virtually any type of material, including that which seems quite nonsensical. However, the more meaningful the material to be learned, the easier it is to memorize. Furthermore, the more meaningful the learned material, the longer it tends to be retained. If a person had sufficient reason for retaining it, a collection of "nonsense" syllables might conceivably be remembered for a lifetime. However, when one develops a reason for retaining something, it no longer is nonsensical.

Memory-level teaching-learning takes the form of either gaining and retaining mentalistic factual materials through mind-training repetitive drills or increasing the probability of desired physicalistic responses through formation of either stimulus-response linkages or response-stimulus reinforcements.[9] So, it seems to exemplify either a mental discipline or a behavioristic theory of learning; either a substantive mind is trained or some relations are formed between stimuli and responses, with no particular thought or purpose being involved. But a cognitive-field psychologist denies that either is

[9] See Robert F. Mager, *Preparing Instructional Objectives* (Palo Alto, Calif.: Fearon Publishers, Inc., 1962).

the case. Instead, he insists that, if anything is learned at all, some degree of insight is always present.

To positive relativists and cognitive-field theorists, what characterizes rote learning is that the insights being acquired have no significant relationship to the material being studied. However, they think that the learned material is *patterned* by the learner during the process of his learning it. Research has shown that even "nonsense syllables," when learned, are not completely unpatterned.[10]

If memorized facts become pertinent to a problem that requires solution, then they contribute to usable background and hence to the effectiveness of problem solving. However, memorized facts usually contribute little to effective student growth. One reason is that they tend to be forgotten quickly. Another is that a large proportion of the facts memorized in school are irrelevant to future thought needs. So, we might even say that the best way to make sure that a student will *not* remember many facts is to place our whole emphasis upon memorized facts.

One might ask, Can the fundamental skills, such as spelling, be taught otherwise than through a process of straight memorization, using drill procedures? Generally speaking, they *can* be taught more efficiently through other procedures. However, much study is required to develop procedures for teaching all the fundamental skill subjects in ways that will free us entirely from rote memorization.

How does a teacher teach for autonomous development?

The contemporary philosophy that champions autonomous development is existentialism. Therefore, this section consists of a very brief description of an existentialist's outlook on pedagogy. An existentialist is concerned with three basic awarenesses and "the teacher's imperative is to arrange the learning situation in such a way as to bring home the truth of these three propositions to every individual."[11] These awarenesses are: I am a *choosing agent*; I am a *free agent;* and I am a *responsible agent.* However, my responsibility is only for how I live my own life. Accordingly, an existentialist teacher is always searching for personal truth. In his teaching, he awakens awareness, freedom, and responsibility in

[10] See George Katona, Organizing and Memorizing (New York: Columbia University Press, 1940).

[11] Van Cleve Morris, *Existentialism in Education* (New York, Harper & Row, Publishers, 1966), p. 135.

his students. But since each person's own feelings are the final authority for the truth that is gained through this process, there is to be no analysis, prescription, or imposition of the activities of anyone by another, including the teacher. All this means that the students as well as the teacher are considered to be autonomously proactive—forwardly active—selves (as opposed to being passive or interactive). Hence teaching proceeds in a completely permissive atmosphere. It actually widens the distance between the teacher and his students, for each develops completely on his own through the exercise of his feelings, and each "does his own thing."

What is understanding-level teaching and learning?

An understanding is a generalized insight in the form of a generalization, concept, principle, rule, theory, or law. Thus, it is the meaningfulness of a region of a life space. Often an understanding may be put into words, but not always. The understandings that a person may achieve in regard to driving a golf ball, timing a motor, flying an airplane, writing a sentence, or developing an educational philosophy may lie in part in a "feel for the act," which would be difficult to verbalize. However, most persons who have thought about such achievements are able to make some statements about both their natures and the probable consequences of attempting them in alternate ways.

Often, when an insight is first "caught," it applies to a single case. Even so, a person is likely to assume that the insight may work in similar situations. Suppose, for example, that after studying a particular situation, one hypothesizes, "Mary became a shoplifter because she felt unwanted by her parents." The natural next step is to think, "Boys and girls who feel unwanted at home tend to become thieves." Of course, this generalization is only *suggested*. It is not *warranted* by the evidence from a single case. Before generalizations become reliable—before they become generalized insights or understandings—it is usually necessary that they rest on a number of specific insights which all suggest the same conclusion. In short, dependable generalizations—understandings—are usually products of considerable experience. Furthermore, in the course of experience, they tend not only to change but also to evolve continuously in the direction of greater usefulness as tools of thought.

An understanding of any thing or process, then, is its generalized meaning. It entails one's ability to use an object, fact, process, or idea in several or even many somewhat different situations. Since it is assumed to be valid in any future situation similar to the ones in which it was tested, it is an *expectation* that enables one to behave intellligently; i.e., with foresight of consequences. So, "to 'understand' something is to make relevant sense of it in some context of human thought, action, or enjoyment in which it can significantly be said to have a meaning."[12]

Syntactically, generalizations are frequently if . . . then statements in the form of "If we take a given action, then the probability is high that a given consequence will follow." Although to behave with foresight we must assume that our generalizations have predictive values, we should also realize that the predictions are always based on probabilities. Positive relativists therefore emphasize that understandings should be regarded as probabilities. However, they recognize that some scientific laws are probabilities so well tested that scientists would be willing to stake their lives on them. In addition to being either verbalized or nonverbalized, highly dependable or only a hunch, an understanding may be either deep, penetrating, and significant, or shallow, superficial, and trivial.

A rather common, though inadequate, meaning of understanding is seeing solitary facts in relation to a general principle. Although understanding, in its fuller sense, means much more than this, teaching would probably be more effective than it now is if all teachers grasped even this limited definition and made understandings, so defined, their goal in teaching. Too few teachers realize that unless students see how items of factual knowledge are embraced by general principles, the facts are quite meaningless.

Because it ignores the role of purpose, understanding as merely seeing relationships is not an adequate concept. Suppose one sees the relationship of certain specific facts to the principle of flotation. A student's reaction to a forced acquaintance with such relationships simply might be "So what?" Accordingly, he would make no attempt either to delve deeply into the implications of the principle, to remember it for future use, or to transfer it to new situations. Consequently, an understanding that is confined to seeing relationships between particulars and a generalization is a fragile and superficial achievement. But suppose a student is a boat hobbyist. He builds boat models and operates them upon a local lake. He is involved in developing a design and needs to know

[12] Arthur E. Murphy, *The Theory of Practical Reason* (LaSalle, Ill.: Open Court Publishing Co., 1964), p. 4.

how much of the boat will submerge when it is carrying four persons whose average weight is 130 pounds. To this student the principle of flotation and the concrete facts subsumed under it become problematic, and consequently will seem of vital importance.

This brings us to a second definition of understanding. We may say that a person understands any object, process, idea, or fact if he sees how it can be used to reach some goal. As soon as a person sees what something is for, he to some degree understands it. Of course, the degree of one's understanding is always relative. If one knows that a camera takes pictures, one has begun to understand a camera. But if the person is going to use a camera successfully, he needs to know the details of its operation and the consequences of using different types of lenses, film emulsions, lighting, and picture compositions.

Note that, according to this second definition, a person's *purpose* is always involved in his understanding. The understander must have a goal, and he must see that which he seeks to understand in relation to that goal. Moreover, he must see how what he is trying to understand can be made to assist in the attainment of the goal, or how it can be kept from hindering such achievement. It is as important to understand things that get in our way as it is to understand those that help us along. A rattlesnake may well be understood as something to be avoided just as a good steak may be understood as something to add savor to life.

If a person really understands a principle, he can probably (1) state it in his own words, (2) give example of it, (3) recognize it in various guises and circumstances, (4) discern the behaviors or lack of behaviors that may represent it, (5) see the relationships between it and other principles or generalizations, (6) see the uses to which it may be put, (7) use it in diverse situations, (8) anticipate the consequences of its application, and (9) state a principle that is opposite to it.

Understanding, then, occurs in its best form when students come to see how to use productively, in ways they care about, a pattern of verified general ideas and the facts that support them. It is important to realize that the concept of understanding as seeing the relation between particulars and generalizations and the concept of understanding as seeing the tool-use of things are highly compatible and mutually complementary ideas. Accordingly, if we are to have an adequate definition of understanding, we must consolidate the two meanings. Thus, "true understanding" or, even better, "functional understanding" is much more likely to occur if a student, in learning generalizations and the specific facts pertinent to them, sees how some purpose is thereby served. So we should not divorce the problem of teaching for understanding from that of promoting student motivation.

According to the outlook of cognitive-field psychology, each individual, when behaving intelligently, is trying cognitively to reconstruct his life space in terms of the way in which its various functional regions—objects and activities—can be made to serve his purposes more effectively. The chief of these purposes is the maintenance and enhancement of one's self. This entails the progressive improvement of the ability to structure and use one's psychological person and environment for one's own purposes. Within such experimental experience, we try first one course of action and then another, preserving only that which works best. It is from such experimentation that our understandings grow.

As soon as one achieves an insight, the thought occurs that possibly this idea will work in other, or all, similar situations. Accordingly, the general value of the insight is tested through its repeated use in similar situations. If it fails to work, it will be discarded because of its extremely limited worth. If it seems always to work, it will become a valued possession that will be added to the person's intellectual makeup—the cognitive structure of his life space. Of course, insights are valid in differing degrees of predictability.

For positive relativists, a defensible understanding-level teaching is teaching that seeks to acquaint students with the relationships between particulars and generalizations—between isolated facts and principles—and simultaneously develops the uses to which the principles may be applied. When a teacher teaches students *rules* governing the use of, say, subjunctives, he is trying to hold his instruction on an understanding level. If he succeeds, his students will be able both to identify cases in which a given rule applies and to use the rule as a guide for his actions.

If a student understands the spelling rules, there is no need for him to be taught the spelling of each particular word. For example, he can be made acquainted with "word families." His understanding of the "at" family enables him to spell bat, cat, fat, gat, etc., or his understanding of the "an" words implements his spelling of can, Dan, fan, man, pan, etc. Likewise, when teachers teach rules for dividing fractions, rules for repairing a motor, or theories in physics, chemistry, or football, they are teaching for understanding.

There are several things that a teacher must do in order to teach effectually on an understanding level. Even before his students arrive, he should have his objectives in terms of generalized insights clearly in mind, and he should have his lesson plans well organized. Then, in teaching, he should exercise productive motivational techniques, use his lesson plans properly, pace the teaching-learning program advantageously, and measure the students' achievement of the objectives in a dispassionate fashion.

A clear contrast may be drawn between understanding-level and memory-level teaching. Whereas memory-level teaching tends to ignore principles or, at best, handles them on such a superficial level that they have no meaning, understanding-level teaching, if successful, gives students not only knowledge of the facts themselves but also insights into the principles by which the facts are related to one another. So, understanding-level teaching-learning equips students with generalized insights, which can be applied in problematic situations both in and outside of school. In this way, it provides them with a mental kit of rules that are tools for their direction of more intelligent behavior. If the rules learned are the best that are known at the time by people in a position to have expert knowledge, students undoubtedly gain a good deal from their education.

Understanding-level teaching, if it remains merely that, casts the students in a passive and the teacher in an active role. The teacher tells and the students listen or the teacher stimulates and the students respond. Thus, understanding-level teaching may be highly uncritical and authoritarian. Furthermore, the principles taught by the teacher may be wrong, and they sometimes are. So, understanding-level teaching may lead to more intelligent behavior on the part of students. But, since it minimizes the purposiveness of students, which is emphasized in cognitive-field psychology, it does not carry with it the development of the quality of experience that is needed to expand intelligence to its fullest potential.

Many advocates of understanding-level teaching, reflecting logical empiricism, have taken for granted that a teacher begins with a body of generalized truths that he (but not the students) knows. Students struggle to learn these truths, with the teacher providing information, motivation, questions, and cues as necessary. The students have successfully completed their learning task when they emerge with an understanding of the predetermined truths that the teacher already knew. So, understanding-level, like memory-level, teaching implies that the teacher purposes, plans, effects, and evaluates the learning product and process that ensue.

This contrasts sharply with reflective-level teaching-learning wherein there is teacher-student cooperative purposing, planning, fulfillment, and evaluation of the classroom procedure and product.

To repeat, for positive relativists, understandings are a person's grasp of how to use productively, in ways which concern him, a pattern of generalized ideas and their supporting facts. Although understandings so defined may be *given* to the student through the efforts of a teacher, a far more productive process is one in which the students and teacher cooperatively formulate some real problems germane to their subject area, then develop the best answers possible to those problems. This is reflecting teaching-learning as it is construed by positive-relativistic educational philosophers.

WHAT ARE REFLECTIVE TEACHING AND LEARNING

When a person reflects, he turns his thoughts back upon an existing idea or article of knowledge that to some degee has been taken to be authentic. Thus, reflection-level teaching-learning is careful, critical examination of an idea or supposed article of knowledge in light of the empirical—testable—evidence that supports it and the further conclusions toward which it points. In other words, it is teacher-student cooperative, exploratory teaching which involves problem development and problem solution. It is based on the conviction of positive relativists, and others, that students study and learn best when they are seeking both the intellectual and emotional relevance of their learning to what they actually need.

A problem, according to positive relativism, is psychological, not ontological; it is immanent, not transcendental, to the stream of experience. It always involves psychological tension in a learner, but it need not be concerned with the characteristics of any absolute reality. In 1949 Dewey wrote, "Whatever relative novelty may be found in my position consists in regarding the problem as belonging in the context of the conduct of inquiry and not in either the traditional ontological or the traditional epistemological context."[13]

[13] John Dewey and Albert G. A. Balz, "A Letter to Mr. Dewey Concerning John Dewey's Doctrine of Possibility, Published Together with His Reply," *The Journal of Philosophy*, vol. 46, no. 11 (May 26, 1949), p. 332.

In the process of reflective teaching, teachers constantly induce students to reconstruct, reorganize, and reinterpret their own experiences. When reflective teaching is successful, students become perplexed to a degree just short of frustration, and they emerge with an enlarged store of generalized insights or understandings and an enhanced ability and desire to develop and solve problems on their own.

Since reflective teaching is problem-centered teaching, what distinguishes reflective from nonreflective understanding-level teaching and learning is the presence of genuine problems that students feel a need to solve. At the outset of a study, a real question develops for which students have no answer, or at least no adequate one. Through the study the students and teacher, working cooperatively, develop what is for them a new or more adequate solution.

There are crucial differences between understanding- and reflection-level teaching. The latter requires, on the part of students, more active participation, more criticism of conventional thinking, and more imagination and creativeness. The classroom atmospheres associated with the two approaches differ markedly. Reflective teaching leads to the development of a classroom atmosphere that is more alive and exciting, more critical and penetrating, and more open to fresh and original thinking. Furthermore, the type of inquiry pursued by a reflective class tends to be more rigorous and "work producing" than that pursued in an understanding-level learning situation.

Reflective-level learning also leads to understandings, but with reflection the search for understandings is pursued in a different fashion from that described in the preceding section. Instead of being given a collection of facts and generalizations by a teacher, students are confronted with something that is problematic—either unclear or puzzling. A student's reflective learning may be based upon the inadequacies or disharmonies of the mental furniture he brings with him to school—his own attitudes, beliefs, values, and knowledge. Or it may begin with some observed inadequacy, inconsistency, incompleteness, or irrelevance in the subject matter or the culture. In any case, if reflective learning occurs, a problematic situation appears on which a student centers his thinking and research. In the reflective process, he examines existing facts and generalizations and seeks out new ones.

To repeat, when reflective teaching is successful, students emerge with an enlarged store of tested insights of a generalized character and an enhanced ability to develop and solve problems on their own. The latter product is as important as the former. If only the first were attained, no claims could be made for reflection-level which could not also be made for understanding-level teaching. However, within genuine problem-centered teaching, students learn the very nature and techniques of problem-solving processes. And if well taught, problem-solving approaches and procedures that are learned in school carry over to be applied to a wide range of problems both in and outside of school.

An understanding of how to solve problems according to principles of scientific reflection is perhaps the most useful intellectual tool a person can possess. If the central goal of education is to foster intelligence, reflective teaching should be the basic approach used by teachers everywhere. One reason why reflective learning is more consistent with the requirements of intelligent behavior is that intelligence usually implies behavior that is active, exploratory, and original. This is not to suggest that intelligent behavior ignores established facts and ideas. It never cuts completely loose from the past. But it does have a tendency to seek something better than what is commonly accepted.

In Chapter 8 we explore how reflective teaching and learning proceed, but first let us see how evaluation contributes to the various types of teaching-learning processes.

HOW DOES EVALUATION CONTRIBUTE TO THE TEACHING-LEARNING PROCESS?

Although there are many different techniques and instruments for evaluating student progress, formalized testing continues to hold a very prominent position among them, particularly in the minds of students. And testing, like teaching, may be conducted on any one of the three levels—memory, understanding, or reflection. (A unique quality of autonomous development is that it cannot be evaluated by anyone other than the learner himself. Thus, student learning can in no way be objectively measured by the teacher.)

When students consider their teachers' evaluation of their achievements, they usually think first of all of tests. Thus, they tend to gauge their level of learning to the level of testing their teacher uses. Consequently, a teacher's program of evaluation not only governs his students' study habits, their manner of interaction in class, and the number and quality of their learnings; it also greatly influences whether they will pursue learning on a memory-, understanding-, or reflection level. The nature of a teacher's system for the evaluation of students' learning has very great influence on the quality of learning actually produced. Even when a teacher strives to teach on an understanding or reflection level, most learning will be on a memory level so long as that is the level on which the teacher tests.

Regardless of the level of learning pursued, students need facts in order to understand anything. Furthermore, they need both facts and understandings in order to learn reflectively. However, positive relativists emphasize that teachers need not be reluctant to experiment with understanding- and reflection-level teaching for fear their students will not learn a sufficient number of facts. When students are taught and tested on the reflection level, they acquire many facts as well as understandings, and likewise when they are taught on the understanding level they acquire much factual information. This process does not, however, work in reverse: there is little about factual learning as such that contributes to understanding, and little about teaching for understanding in a nonreflective way that contributes to a student's reflective powers and habits.[14]

How is memory-level learning tested?

Memory-level learning may be either mentalistic-factual or physicalistic-behavioral learning. In mentalistic testing, factual essay or short-answer tests are employed to check for recall of retained memories. Students' answers are checked against a list prepared when the test was made.

In testing for learned physicalistic behaviors, the teacher takes a sampling of the behavioral modification included in a statement of behavioral objectives which was developed prior to the beginning of the course. These modifications all are in the form of observable responses.

How is understanding-level learning evaluated?

Either factual and explanatory essay tests or short-answer true-false, selection or completion tests are most appropriate for testing students' understandings that are learned on an understanding

[14] See Ernest E. Bayles, *Democratic Educational Theory* (New York: Harper & Row, Publishers, 1960), especially chap. 1, "Experiments with Reflective Teaching."

level. Through the use of these, students demonstrate how well they can recognize, explain, or use the understandings or generalized insights that the teacher has expected them to acquire.

In testing on an understanding level the teacher checks students' answers against a prepared list of answers. However (and here the process differs from that of memory-level testing), as long as the answers are correct the teacher credits students for "right" answers even though they use wording somewhat different from that of the instructor.

What is unique about reflective-level evaluation?

Any discussion of reflective-level evaluation might seem to fit best at the close of Chapter 8, on reflective-level procedures. However, a brief introduction to this process is included here so that readers can see that there really is something significantly different about reflective teaching and evaluation.

Since reflective teaching entails problem-centered, exploratory personal involvement, testing which is compatible with it will likewise be centered on genuine problems. When one is teaching on a reflective level he should be trying, in testing as well as in all other evaluational procedures, to find out whether the individual student is able to apply adequate information to the solution of a problem in such a way as to harmonize the problem, all available pertinent data or facts, and the answer. The most practicable instruments for the accomplishment of this purpose are problem-centered essay tests. A reflective-level essay test usually consists of four, three, or even fewer carefully constructed questions. Each question should be pertinent to the study which the students have been pursuing and should constitute a real problem for them.

The best type of reflective-level question is one to which there is possibly more than one true answer. So, answers cannot be written out at the time the test is constructed. Each answer must be evaluated on its own merits. In an adequate answer many facts will be used, but the number of facts listed as such will not be the basis for evaluation. Instead, answers will be evaluated on the basis of some criteria—measuring sticks—that the teacher and students have agreed upon prior to the test. Probably, these criteria will be *adequacy* of the pertinent data that are applied to the solution of the problem, *harmony* of the problem, data, and answer, and perhaps one or two others.

A positive relativist would neither test his students on a memory level nor use so-called false-true tests. He prefers to use essay tests, and he strives to make his questions truly reflective ones. At times he may use selection tests, but he will realize that in so doing he is drawing his student away from reflective thinking. Nevertheless, he is still holding his teaching and testing to an understanding level; this is acceptable, but not ideal.

How are reflective teaching and learning accomplished?

The primary goal of reflective teaching is the promotion of reflective learning in both the students and the teacher. Reflective learning requires time and either a series of life spaces or a life space of some duration. It includes casting, elaborating, and testing hypotheses. It arises in a situation—life space—wherein a person feels a need—has a goal. In place of a clear path to the goal he perceives a forked road, a barricaded road, or no road at all. So a problem presents itself as an unclear, inadequately structured life space.

It is through reflective thinking that a person accomplishes reflective learning: through changing his perception of the total situation he restructures and transforms his current life space and provides for potential changes of future life spaces. Through productive reflective thinking an individual achieves effective changes in the cognitive structure of his life space; he gains new insights and changes old ones. Progress in thinking means that a person has attained the capacity to approach the solution of a problem by a new, more productive path. The products of reflective teaching and learning are tested generalized insights—generalizations; they have the attributes of rules, principles, or laws.

A person who experiences reflective learning should thereby gain an increased store of generalized insights related to the subject studied; and these should be incorporated at the personality level so that a permanent change in him occurs. Furthermore, he should show a greater disposition and ability to apply the method of scientific reflection to problems outside the school subject in which reflective learning occurs.

HOW WELL DOES REFLECTIVE TEACHING APPLY TO THE DIFFERENT SUBJECT MATTER FIELDS?

Many teachers see problem-centered, reflective teaching as a possible approach to instruction in a limited number of courses, such as social studies, literature, industrial arts, and home economics, but often they are unable to imagine its use in the teaching of such subjects as mathematics, physics, music, physical education, and foreign language. Nevertheless, the essential characteristics of reflective teaching have enough flexibility to be employed in all school subjects, including those which seem on the surface to encompass only cut-and-dried subject matter.

Problem-centered teaching is something which grows out of a unique relationship between the teacher and his students rather than in conjunction with the specific nature of formal course materials. It springs into existence in those situations where the minds of teacher and students are cooperatively engaged. Consequently, it emerges whenever a teacher, through adroit questioning and use of negative evidence, induces students either to doubt what they have accepted up to now or to wonder about something which hitherto has been of no concern to them. It continues as the teacher helps the students analyze reflectively the issues that have arisen. In most conventional school subjects, opportunities regularly appear for a teacher to operate in this manner. Passages in a textbook, assertions made by students, a news story, a motion picture or television show—any of these may serve at times as a springboard for the creation of problems.

Some courses and some types of course organization seem to lend themselves more readily to reflective teaching than do others. A course that has been construed broadly—that is, whose subject matter is not narrowly prescribed—probably is a better medium for reflection than is a more narrow course. Thus, as usually defined, general business is a better course for reflection-level teaching than is shorthand; problems of democracy better than economic geography; history and philosophy of mathematics better than algebra; and world literature better than freshman composition. This difference is not, however, inherent in the nature of the subject matter as such. It lies in the frame of reference within which the students are customarily treated and the social atmosphere that pervades the teaching-learning situation.

A course within which problem-centered teaching is pursued cannot be bound rigidly to a textbook. Real problems are psychological; data used in solving them are rarely organized in the same pattern as are textbooks and courses of study. The "logical" organization of the subject matter of a book as it is arranged in the mind of an authority in the field simply does not, as a rule, coincide with the course taken by the growing minds of students. Hence, subjects are best adapted to reflective teaching when they are allowed to cut across subject-matter lines whenever this makes sense in terms of the particular problem being studied. This is perhaps the most defensible rationale for a core curriculum. Furthermore, since much of the content of the textbooks presently available tends to be irrelevant to critical analyses of ideas, attitudes, and beliefs, reflective problems can be best handled if a teacher is not required to follow a textbook too closely.

Determination of which subjects, or which topics within a subject, should be handled as problems cannot be made without reference to the specific classroom situation. In each case, the teacher should take into account the maturity and experiential background of students, the attitudes that prevail in the community, his own preparation and skill, and the anticipated consequences of having the class delve deeply into the subject.

There is a growing body of evidence that every subject-matter area on every level from kindergarten to college graduate classes has been and is being taught reflectively, at least by a minority of teachers. (See pages 172–174, whch list references to reflective teaching.) Consequently, positive relativists are convinced that reflection-level can become the prevailing mode of teaching and learning, provided teachers and students become convinced that it is the most advantageous level on which to operate.

HOW EFFECTIVE IS REFLECTIVE TEACHING?

It might seem logical to assume that, on a test designed to measure recall of facts, students taught on a memory or an understanding level would fare better than those taught reflectively. However, if we are to take at face value a group of studies extending from 1940 into the 1950s, this is apparently not the case. These studies, all designed to test the results of reflective teaching, have been reported by Bayles.[1]

The studies were conducted by public school teachers in Kansas and Missouri and culminated in the form of master's theses. Four of the six studies reported were conducted in high school social studies and the other two in fifth- and sixth-grade classes.

The general procedure was as follows: Students were given IQ tests to determine the average IQ of a class. Only those classes which were approximately "average" were used. Then so far as the teachers were able to do it, the classes were taught reflectively. The teachers measured the effects of reflective instruction by giving various standardized achievement tests and by observing such changes of students' overt behavior as made it possible to infer the quality of their learning.

The control group used in evaluation of test results was in each case the group upon which the test had been standardized. All tests used had been standardized on groups of students of average IQ or better. The control against which teachers judged student behavior was much more subjective—the behavior of students of

[1] "Experiments with Reflective Teaching," *Kansas Studies in Education*, April 1956. This monograph is reproduced in essentially its original form in Ernest E. Bayles, *Democratic Educational Theory* (New York: Harper & Row, Publishers, 1960), chap. 1.

other classes which the teachers had taught in conventional fashion. However, since each of the teachers was experienced and able, the subjective impressions they reported were considered worthy of respect.

The results of each study were very clear-cut. Irrespective of whether the achievement tests emphasized fact recall or the application of principles, students who had been taught reflectively scored conspicuously higher than the national or regional norms in almost all cases. Those who did not actually score higher than the norms made exceptionally large gains during the school term. With respect to informally gathered data, teachers reported the following results: (1) heightened interest apparent among students; (2) more work done; (3) more voluntary reporting of data encountered outside school (gathered from radio, newspapers, magazines, etc.); (4) increased tendency to be critical—to demand evidence; (5) increased participation in discussions, particularly on the part of students formerly reticent; and (6) much more reading. Some of the teachers obtained librarians' records of magazines and books checked out by students; they found that the students in their reflectively taught classes were reading more than any others in school.

To determine the gain achieved during a term, one of the investigators continued for a period of six years to give achievement tests to respective classes at the beginning and end of each school term. She found that the net gain in learning increased from year to year. This indicated that with continued experience with reflective teaching a teacher becomes more effective in his teaching role. If the six teachers participating in these studies had had several years of reflective teaching experience behind them (most were trying it for the first time) it seems likely that the studies would have revealed even more spectacular results.

Many teachers think that reflective teaching succeeds only with the best students, but one of the studies reported by Bayles suggests that this is not true. In the instance reported, reflective teaching was used in a class containing a wide range of ability: students of low ability made greater percentage gains than did those of high ability. However, the investigator concluded that her teaching had not been pitched on a level high enough to present a challenge to the superior group. Probably a safe conclusion is that reflective teaching, when effective, tends to bring students of all levels of ability up to maximum, or near maximum, performance.

HOW IS THINKING RELATED TO LEARNING?

Since we achieve reflective learning through reflective thinking, a key problem germane to an understanding of reflective teaching involves the relationship of thinking to learning. Each philosophic school has its characteristic definition and understanding of the nature of the thinking process, and each in some way associates thinking with learning. Both idealists and rational realists conceive thinking to be a process discharged by an active, rational, substantive mind. So their interpretations of thinking are quite similar. However, they differ in that, whereas idealists emphasize the individual's living his way into his system of thinking, rational realists teach that he should think his way rationally into a system of living. But, for both idealists and rational realists, thinking is the process whereby an active, subjective mind reads meaning into the universe through rational development of its coherent conceptual structure. Within the thinking process, a finite mentalistic self uses its cognitive faculties to attune itself to an infinite spiritual reality.

Both logical empiricists and positive relativists construe thinking within a scientific psychological frame of reference, but in very different manners. In order to bring into sharper focus the meaning which thinking has for positive relativists, we first describe how logical empiricists deal with the subject.

Within logical-empiricistic behaviorism, what is thinking?

For most behaviorists, an "idea" or "thought" consists of a symbolic movement that constitutes an intermediate step between overt stimuli and responses. *Symbols* are events that represent something beyond themselves. They may be either substitute stimuli or substitute responses. Whenever an organism is responding in a certain way, and the stimulus that was originally adequate to evoke the response is absent, the organism is responding to a symbolic stimulus. A symbolic response in an incipient—partial—movement that takes the place of a completely expressed pattern of behavior. It may take the form of a shrug of the shoulders, a facial expression, a nod of the head, or a change in posture. In thinking, symbolic movements may be so slight that the individual may be aware of only a "thought" divorced from any movement.

Nevertheless, behaviorists believe that when one thinks, at least some slight muscular, glandular, or organic action does occur.

Man's thinking, then, is his behaving symbolically or incipiently in a random, trial-and-error fashion. Thought is not some mentalistic process that is the cause of behavior, but the behavior itself. Thus, thinking is symbolic or incipient trial-and-error behavior that culminates in learning. Like all other instances of an organism's behavior, it is a function or result of a set of antecedent conditions.

In thinking, an organism makes symbolic miniature responses which sample the feedbacks that would occur if the actions represented symbolically or incipiently were really carried out. Thus, to behaviorists, thought consists of very small preparatory responses. So construed, thinking can be observed in the incipient or miniature trial-and-error movements of a rat at a "choice point" in a maze. Here small movements, this way and that, often precede the rat's actually moving down a pathway. In human being this process is subtle and more elaborated, but it is no different in kind from that of rats and other lower animals.

In its broadest sense, thinking behavior is both verbal and nonverbal, both overt and covert. However, any nonverbal or covert aspects of behavior are considered to function much like the observable ones; they too are segments of stimulus-response sequences. Accordingly, behaviorists assume that, once natural laws governing the relationship of observable stimuli and responses are identified and established, internal processes likewise can be described in terms of stimulus-response sequences, which conform to the same laws. Thus, ideational thought—a variable that intervenes between observable stimuli and responses—likewise consists of stimuli and responses, albeit covert ones.

Although B. F. Skinner and some others consider the study of any private, internal events irrelevant to a functional analysis of behavior, many other contemporary behaviorists follow John B. Watson's earlier leadership in regarding thinking as basically a matter of implicit speech—talking to oneself. Thus, they associate thought very closely with language, which is a rich collection of symbols. So considered, thought is basically a laryngeal activity mediated by a nervous system. However, it is closely aligned with gestures, frown, shrugs, and grimaces that symbolize, that is, take the place of more overt actions or behaviors.

In the thinking process, words, other symbols, and incipient movements become *cues* for behavior. Cues are stimuli of faint intensity that evoke or guide an organism's movements. Any uniqueness man may have involves his "better" use of cues. Three principal factors make man's thinking processes "higher" than those of other animals. First, man has greater capacity to respond selectively to more subtle aspects of the environment as cues. Secondly, he is able to make a greater variety of distinctive responses that constitute cues for his actions, i.e., he is more able to stimulate himself. Finally, he can emit a greater number of cue-responses simultaneously. Thus, he can elicit many more of his own future responses based on patterns of cues that represent, or result from, several different earlier patterns of stimulation.[2]

How do positive relativists conceive of thinking as being a reflective process?

Positive relativists are convinced that any change in insight is invariably accompanied by some degree of thought, and that thought always produces some change, however slight, in insight. Thus, in their view, learning and thought are closely related. Furthermore, they consider thinking to be a reflective activity within which a person develops new or changed insights through a process of casting, elaborating, and testing hypotheses. In other words, they do not regard thinking as a case of "spontaneous combustion." Instead, they think that thought is a reflective process which originates only in relation to some perplexity, confusion, or doubt experienced within the life space of a person. A reflective process is the "active, persistent, and careful consideration of any belief or supposed form of knowledge in the light of the grounds that support it, and the further conclusions to which it tends. . . ."[3]

A positive relativist thinks that there is no essential difference between reflective thinking and relativistic scientific processes broadly defined. However, the term *scientific* does carry a connotation that is less suited to general educational purposes than is the sense conveyed by the term *reflective*. In the thinking of many persons, *science* implies white-gowned technicians, microscopes and telescopes, chemical tables, and cyclotrons. Furthermore, it suggests precise measurement, use of mathematics, a large amount of rather esoteric wizardry, and neglect of moral values. But, *scientific* in its broadest sense covers not only a spe-

[2] See Sigmund Koch, ed., *Psychology: A Study of a Science*, vol. 2, *General Systematic Formulations, Learning, and Special Processes* (New York: McGraw-Hill Book Company, 1959), p. 247.

[3] John Dewey, *How We Think* (Lexington, Mass.: D. C. Heath & Company, 1933), p. 9.

cial kind of gadgetry and techniques but also a unique outlook, attitude, method of inquiry, and approach to values.

Reflection, then, refers to the essential features of the scientific method broadly conceived. It implies an attitude of mind and a generalized set of operations with which men may approach all problems, whether physical, social, moral, or psychological in nature. Hence all thinking that is worthwhile is reflection, as we herein define it. Furthermore, reflection leads to the development of kinds of generalizations that are understood by learners and have, at the same time, maximum transfer value for new situations.

Within reflective experience, thinking and the objects of thought are never separated from one another or from problematic situations. "Since thought always proceeds by way of unraveling some doubt or solving some problem, and knowledge is the outcome of thought, to present the knowledge without the problems that it arose to meet is to ask the student to shake hands with a scarecrow."[4]

Five rather definite aspects are present in each complete act of reflective thinking. However, no one should suppose that a person goes through them in any one consecutive, orderly fashion. Any or even all of the aspects may develop concurrently, or any aspect may precede another. The five aspects should never, therefore, be taken to be successive steps in reflective thinking. Moreover, teachers should recognize that any reflective process is normally characterized by confusion, hesitation, backtracking, and "going around in circles." Reflective thinking is seldom easy. At its best, it is exhilarating and exciting; at its worst, it is painfully hard work beset with many frustrations.

The principal aspects of reflective thinking are as follows.

1. Recognition and definition of a problem. This occurs when one becomes aware either of conflicting goals, of conflicting paths to a goal, or of a goal and an intervening obstacle—a barrier—to its achievement. Often a problem consists of a newly sensed discrepancy in known data.
2. Formulation of hypotheses. Hypotheses are invented generalizations—possible answers—that to be used most successfully must be verified by human experience. In a relativistic sense, all scientific generalizations are hypotheses in which greater or lesser degrees of confidence can be placed. They range from hunches based on a minimum of data to laws, which reflect a very high degree of factual verification.

[4] Robert S. Brumbaugh and Nathaniel M. Lawrence, *Philosophers on Education* (Boston: Houghton Mifflin Company, 1963), p. 142.

3. Elaboration of logical implications of hypotheses. This includes both deducing the implications or consequences concerning which observations have already been made, so that hypotheses may be checked against present knowledge, and deducing further implications or consequences concerning which observations have not yet been made, so that the hypotheses may be tested through research and experiments still to be designed and applied.
4. Testing or verification of hypotheses. This involves attempts to verify the implications or consequences deduced within the process of the third aspect. Verification is accomplished through both *scrutiny-explanation* and *prediction-verification* processes. In scrutiny-explanation, one uses the data of previous experience to verify a hypothesis. In prediction-verification, ones uses new data that are procured through making experimental tests.
5. Drawing conclusions. This consists of either acceptance, modification, or rejection of the hypotheses, or of concluding that as of now the available pertinent evidence does not warrant taking any stand at all.[5]

HOW MAY AN APPROPRIATE CLASSROOM ATMOSPHERE PROMOTE REFLECTIVE LEARNING?

The most important feature of reflective teaching and learning is a classroom atmosphere within which there is a genuine desire for teacher-student cooperative learning through the use of research procedures. A teacher's success in inducing reflective learning in students hinges upon his ability to bring them to involve themselves in significant issues to the point of perplexity and yet to keep themselves curious and open-minded in regard to solution of each issue. This section of the chapter deals with some means whereby students may be brought to be deeply involved without becoming frustrated. It also explores ways in which students can be influenced to become more receptive to basing knowledge upon empirical, scientific evidence.

The type of atmosphere within which a person feels sufficiently secure to dare entertain evidence which contradicts his current

[5] The formulation presented here is more or less standard, and its essential form appears in many writings. The specific way in which the steps appear here was suggested to the author by Ernest E. Bayles.

knowledge and values seems most readily attainable in face-to-face groups wherein warmth and trust have been deliberately cultivated. Some techniques that a teacher may employ to create such an atmosphere include (1) reduction of threat and promotion of open-mindedness, (2) encouragement of group membership, and (3) practice of democratic group leadership in fostering group decisions.

How may a teacher reduce threat and promote open-mindedness in students?

Several techniques are available for keeping a sense of threat to a minimum and thereby increasing students' open-mindedness. First of all, a teacher should always treat the student's ideas and opinions with respect. This does not mean that he must express approval of every thought a student expresses; but he should strive to avoid ridicule and sarcasm, or any kind of statement that might be interpreted as such. Furthermore, when students offer serious observations or opinions, the teacher should in no way disparage their intelligence, wisdom, or motivation. Statements that are offered in good faith should be taken for what they are—the best insights students are able to muster. Consequently, no matter how ill-formed or unorthodox a student's ideas may seem to be, he should feel complete freedom to express them without being threatened in any way.

Another technique for reduction of threat and promotion of open-mindedness is to arrange learning situations so that facts "speak for themselves." Other things being equal, facts—especially when they are impersonal, sharply relevant, and simple enough to be easily grasped—are more likely to break through an emotional barrier than are expressions of opinion. In most teaching-learning situations, therefore, it pays to minimize, or at least not encourage, emphasis upon merely personal opinions. Instead, the learning enterprise should focus on questions concerning what will come of acting in accordance with a given proposition or hypothesis. In this way issues may be handled as issues and propositions discussed on their own merits. A teacher may convert an opinion into a proposition simply by saying: "Here is an opinion that is before the class. Let us take it as a proposition to be tested. If it is true, what consequences may we deduce from it?" Experiments cited by Lewin[6] suggest that, when a group is presented

[6] See Kurt Lewin, "Group Decision and Social Change," in Theodore Newcomb and Eugene Hartley, ed., *Readings in Social Psychology* (New York: Holt, Rinehart and Winston, Inc., 1947), pp. 330–344.

with a problem to discuss, ideas and behaviors contrary to those accepted by group members are more likely to be entertained seriously, and later adopted, if the problem is discussed with reference to persons other than themselves—at least in the early phases of a discussion.

When a teacher does challenge an idea or opinion expressed by a student, he should do it in such a way that the existing ideological conflict is internalized. That is, the student is made to feel the conflict within his own personality or life space. If he sees the conflict merely as a contest between himself and someone else, he will probably not frame a problem in regard to it. So, when a teacher wishes to contest an idea or opinion of a student, he is well advised to handle it somewhat like this: "You have your position and I think I understand and appreciate your reasons. But there are contrary ideas that are widely held by other competent people. I wonder if there is any merit in a point of view such as . . . ?" Thus, the students is asked to entertain and evaluate, not the outlook of the teacher or a classmate, but simply a position, conflicting with his own, that some people hold.

How may a teacher encourage group membership?

Whether it is achieved simply through classroom informality or by deliberately fostered out-of-school contacts, there are sound pedagogical advantages in students' becoming well acquainted with one another. A deep-seated desire of human beings is for security, and a common means of a person's achieving security is through his acquiring membership in a group. When a person feels that he has a place in a group, that he "fits in," that he is wanted, he feels secure. As Lewin pointed out, "The social climate in which a child lives is for the child as important as the air it breathes. The group to which a child belongs is the ground on which he stands. His relation to the group and his status in it are the most important factors for his feeling of security or insecurity."[7] Students who are members of a group of individuals making the same changes together are more likely to abandon some of their prejudices, change their insights, and revise their values than are individuals who are doing their thinking in isolation.

Individuals are rarely, if ever, completely subject to group con-

[7] Kurt Lewin, *Resolving Social Conflicts* (New York: Harper & Row, Publishers, 1948), p. 82.

trol, nevertheless, there is little likelihood that a person will make significant changes in his ideology and practices on his own, outside his relationship with his primary group. Still, he may develop an idea or value that is novel to his group and gradually obtain its acceptance by other members, until in time it becomes effective in influencing the behavior of the group.

Encouragement of full and free communication among its members will heighten the cohesiveness of a group. If students understand each other, they will almost inevitably work together better as a group. A teacher should urge and help students to state opinions and propositions meaningfully. Also, he should discourage use of emotive language, particularly when students are inclined to direct personal gibes at each other. Furthermore, he should make certain that every group member has a chance to be heard and have his statements correctly interpreted.

In establishing group feeling, there are possible advantages to be gained from subgroup study and projects. However, when this sort of operation is attempted, it is best to divide a class into small groups and to see that the same students do not always work together. A student-committee system can work fairly well in gathering information, but its effectiveness in reflective evaluation of data and productive solution of problems depends on the maturity of the students and their familiarity with the rules of reflection. Generally speaking, if reflective deliberation is highly productive, a teacher is usually a central figure in the process.

Cliques, self-contained groupings based on religious or social-class affiliations, racial groupings, or associations based on levels of academic achievement may develop within any school and be reflected in subgroups within a single classroom. Such groupings may entirely exclude certain students who in turn become social isolates. With the development of subgroups of this sort, especially if blindly patriotic group attitudes are involved, a class may become badly split and team spirit may become difficult to achieve. Hence, if either his personal observations or his use of sociometric devices suggests to a teacher that an unhealthy social situation exists in his classroom, he should take steps to alleviate it.[8]

[8] One of the most useful references on the means of analyzing the social structure of groups and the techniques to use in establishing greater cohesiveness is Helen Hall Jennings, *Sociometry in Group Relations: A Work Guide for Teachers* (Washington, D.C.: American Council on Education, 1949).

How does a teacher practice democratic leadership in fostering group decisions?

The aim of democratic group leadership is to translate a democratic philosophy into group action. In Chapter 6 we defined democracy as a social arrangement within which all members of a group share equally in determining which freedoms and restraints shall apply. It is presumed that, in general, freedoms and restraints shall apply with the same force to all. But democracy must allow for the granting of special powers for special purposes (as in the case of its executive officers). If we think of democracy as a system of *equally limited* freedoms, characterized by shared decisions regarding which specific rules are to prevail, then we have a clear criterion for distinguishing democratic from other types of social arrangements. A social system may provide for *unlimited freedoms,* in which case it is called anarchy. It may provide for *unequally limited* freedoms, in which case it is called autocracy. Or, it may provide for *equally limited freedoms,* in which case it is called democracy.

A teacher, as a democratic group leader, asserts his leadership in harmony with the processes that should prevail within a democratic group. Since a democratic group is self-governed, it must provide for situations wherein disagreements occur. Ideally, democratic decisions are by consensus, i.e., mutually agreeable decisions reached through discussion and concession. Then, by common consent, action is taken. However, if it is time for action to occur and a consensus is not yet possible, a democratic group votes. Each person has an equal vote, and a majority vote wins. So votes are taken to facilitate action, not to enforce views, outlooks, or opinions.

The successful and enduring operation of democracy requires that a group maintain certain conditions which, although not central to the idea of democracy, contribute to its functioning. If participation is to be full and free, a group must establish a hospitable atmosphere—one within which every member is considered important. Democratic participation implies reasonable freedom of communication and freedom of speech and thought. So, *all* opinions must be guaranteed a hearing. If any single individual or minority group gains disproportionate control over agencies of communication and opinion, the society has lost equality of participation in decision making.

Also, if a democratic society is to survive over time, a majority

of its members must learn to make reflective decisions whenever socially important questions are involved. A democratic society assumes competence on the part of its members; any different assumption would lead to distrust and rejection of the principle of equal participation. Without wise leadership no society can solve its problems and endure. However, in a democracy wise leadership arises through wise citizenship. So, if democracy is to survive, its members must take steps to insure that the principle of reflection is employed as widely as possible in making choices regarding matters of group concern.

Behavior of a group is influenced significantly by its leaders. However, the role of democratic leadership is to help a group realize its own potentialities for growth. If a group is immature, its overall emotional and intellectual climate as well as its direction and extent of growth depend largely on the conduct of its leadership. But as a group matures, it becomes less dependent on any particular leader. Instead, it develops the capacity to produce leaders from its own ranks and to reject and select leaders according to emerging group needs.

No matter how great their internal rapport, groups do not change their ideas automatically. Still, a most effectual instrument for producing group ideological changes is a democratically led discussion. Probably the most important requirement of discussion, or other modes of study designed to change people's basic insights or attitudes, is that it have the quality of genuine self-learning. Since students often resist outside pressure to change their ideas, the object of democratic leadership is not to apply pressure from outside but to remove counterforces within individuals and groups.

Although a teacher can, and usually must, help in eliminating these counterforces, students must perform the actual removal, each within his own life space. If they can explore a problem independently, feeling no authoritarian pressure from above to explore it in a particular way or to emerge with particular conclusions, they are much more likely than otherwise to undergo real and permanent changes in conceptual patterns. Consequently, they need to be encouraged to use investigatory techniques of their own, and to explore by themselves provocative readings, trips, interviews, and radio and television programs. A teacher's role here is to suggest possible directions of exploration and to help students evaluate the facts that are exposed.

If the facts come to students in real life situations, it may only

be necessary to remind the students of their relevance and their bearing on the problem at hand. For example, a trip to a slum may speak eloquently against the notion that everyone is adequately housed, or the witnessing of a Congressional investigation over television may show quite convincingly that traditional American principles of fair play are not always employed. Kurt Lewin has stated that "an individual will believe facts he himself has discovered in the same way he believes in himself or in his group."[9]

For a maximum change in students' insights to occur, the students need to communicate their views to each other, so that the thinking and intentions of each are known to all. When it becomes evident to dissident individuals that most members of a group have revised their outlooks and expect to change their behaviors accordingly, the dissidents may find change within their own thinking somewhat easier to achieve. So, reflective discussion of problems should culminate in group decisions. That is, in addition to discussing and studying a problem, students as a group should consider what conclusions are warranted, what the conclusions mean to them, and what, if anything, they intend to do about them.

HOW ARE THOROUGHNESS AND ORDERLINESS RELATED TO REFLECTIVE TEACHING?

Positive relativists stress two basic points regarding the overall process of reflective, problem-centered study. One relates to thoroughness, the other to orderliness.

Thoroughness and reflective teaching

When a teacher and a class of ninth-graders purport to "solve" some highly difficult problem during the course of a unit of study covering a period of, say, only three days, the procedure has probably been a travesty on education. It is conceivable that in this length of time students might inform themselves a little better or push their thinking forward a little more. But to talk about their achieving solutions so quickly is nonsense. Truly problem-centered teaching, like any teaching that leads to under-

[9] *Resolving Social Conflicts,* p. 68.

standing, is necessarily an unhurried procedure. Consequently it is very difficult, and usually impossible, to pursue problem-centered teaching in situations that are characterized by rigid scheduling of time or units to be covered.

To make problem-centered teaching a success, a teacher may need to make several false starts; when one plan for bringing students to help formulate a problem fails, he tries another, until finally he hits on one that works. The period during which a given problem is studied is necessarily rather unstructured, and frequently it is impossible to predict how soon a class will devise anything resembling an answer. Even though a problem has been under study a week or more and nothing educational seems to have happened, so long as the teacher thinks there is still a good chance that some useful insights will emerge, study should be continued. Yet, teachers should recognize that, in education, something like a "law of diminishing returns" operates; in connection with each problem, a time is reached when further pursuit of the problem will obviously not be worth the time and effort involved. It is then time to move to another inquiry.

The length of time students will struggle with a problem depends upon their age and maturity. First-graders need to come to a conclusion soon after they develop a problem, perhaps the same day. But college seniors may accomplish their best learning when they struggle with a problem for a semester or longer. The high school inquiry concerning the meaning of *race,* introduced on page 163, should occupy a class daily for at least two weeks.

Most textbooks and courses of study contain entirely too many topics for each to be treated in a problem-centered fashion. Consequently, teachers who wish to experiment with problem-centered teaching must free themselves somewhat from the dictates of standard printed guides and textbooks. This does not necessarily mean ignoring such guides (which is seldom possible anyway); rather, they should be used judiciously, with clear recognition that they need not, and should not, be followed literally.

Orderliness and reflective teaching

Problem-centered study is rarely, if ever, as orderly as written descriptions of it might imply. To realize this, one need only to listen carefully to a group discussion of some matter about which most members of the group have a sizable personal concern. Hypotheses are advanced, evidence is stated, and conclusions are suggested in what, on the surface, appears to be a random order. Thought, even for the best-organized persons, is seldom completely ordered in a one-two-three fashion. Although we list a series of aspects involved in reflective thinking and learning that correspond to aspects of scientific procedure, they are rarely, as we have noted, taken as steps in any logical order. A thinker moves continuously back and forth from problem to hypotheses to evidence to conclusions in a varying order. Furthermore, at any given moment a new idea may strike him in so sharp a focus that it sets off an entirely different train of thought, sometimes about a quite different problem.

Despite the inevitable appearance of disorderliness that characterizes most highly motivated discussions, a teacher is obligated to preside in such way as to see that appropriate questions get asked, that obvious hypotheses are not ignored, that pertinent evidence is not glossed over, and that relevant conclusions are presented and debated. In short, it is his duty to see that all aspects of reflective study are evidenced at some time during the discussion. Only then will individual students have available for their private reflection all that a group study situation can contribute.

In the next and last section of the book we describe how reflective teaching and learning proceed. To bring the presentation into sharper focus we align the appropriate aspects of an actual teaching unit with a discussion of the teaching-learning process. However, readers are reminded that it is impossible for an instructor to teach reflectively by drawing up the blueprints of his classroom operation and then following them explicitly.

When truly reflective learning occurs, each class, to some degree, proceeds differently from any that have preceded or any that will follow it. A teacher should have in mind, and even on paper, the anticipated outcome of his class's inquiry, but these never should be specific objectives toward which the students are either led or driven. The way should always be left open for conclusions different from those anticipated by the teacher. The teacher should only insist that all conclusions are based on adequate, testable evidence.

WHAT IS A PROBLEM?

In reflective or problem-centered classes, instruction begins with introduction of an "I don't know" or problematic situation—one in which students are faced with a question they cannot answer.

Ideal problems for classroom study involve situations which are sufficiently complex to be challenging, yet simple enough to make it possible for most students in a class to formulate and test some hypotheses that may lead to a solution. A problem should, in other words, be so compelling that students really want to study it, but not so overwhelming that they are inclined to give up. A study should generate an urge to analyze the possible obstacles and dilemmas in the situation, to understand them, and to devise means for resolving the difficulties. After aiding students in raising a problem, the teacher helps them investigate it until an answer is found. Problem solving consists of formulating hypotheses and testing them with all the pertinent evidence available. Facts are therefore gathered in profusion, but teachers should make no attempt to encourage fact learning or fact recall *as such* merely for the sake of accumulating facts.

When is a problem a problem?

Too many teachers who have attempted a problems approach to teaching have not adequately understood the psychology of learning as it relates to problem-centered study. Often "problem-centered teaching" has failed because what teachers have chosen as "problems" have not actually been problems in a psychological sense. Contributions of cognitive-field psychologists enable us to understand better what happens to a person psychologically when he has a problem. A learning problem is neither an impersonal, objective issue to be resolved nor a task of busywork. Instead, for a "problem" to be a problem, it must involve *psychological tension in a learner.*

How is a problem a felt tension?

To have a problem, a person must first have a goal or goals that he accepts as his own. Then, a problem arises when he finds it impossible to proceed quickly and directly to the goal. When he cannot achieve his goal readily, it is because he either sees no open path to it or sees two or more competing paths, or two or more competing goals, and cannot decide which to pursue. Cognitive-field concepts and terminology are especially useful in expressing the basic elements of problematic situations. (At this point readers should review the basic ideas of cognitive-field psychology, which are presented in Chapter 2, pages 16–21, and Chapter 5, pages 74–88.)

When a person is confronted with a problem, either there is

Barrier or no-path situation

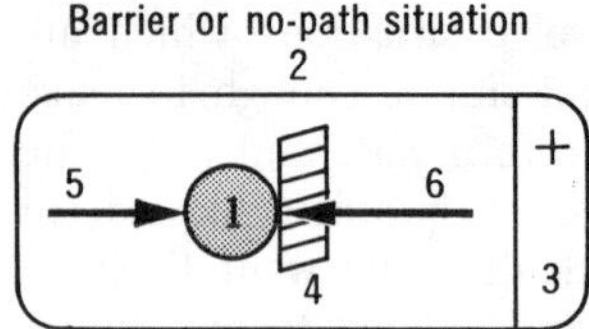

1. Person
2. Boundary of psychological environment
3. Goal; region of positive valence
4. Barrier
5. Vector of driving force toward goal
6. Vector of restraining force of barrier

Conflicting-path situations

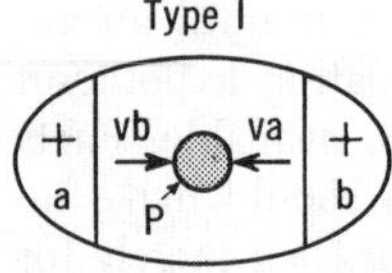

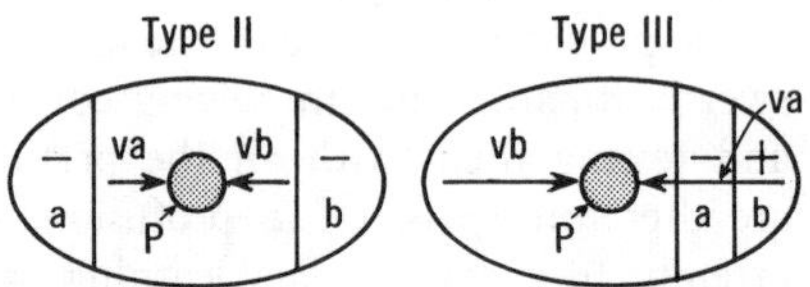

FIGURE 8. Field-conflict situations.

a goal region in his life space that has a positive valence and a barrier between his person and the region of positive valence, or there are several conflicting goal regions toward which or away from which he might want to make psychological movement. These two general types of situations are barrier, or no-path, situations and conflicting-path situations and are shown in Figure 8.

Conflicting-path situations lend themselves best to reflective or problem-centered teaching. In a Type I situation, a person has two conflicting goals or two opposite regions of his life space both with positive valences. (Positive-goal regions being opposite means that both cannot be achieved at the same time.) In the Type I illustration, vector vb represents a psychological force equal to the valence of region b, and vector va represents a force equal to the valence of region a. In a Type II situation, the person is faced with two opposite significant regions of his life space, each having a negative valence; he wants to escape both, and they are of such nature that this is impossible. In a Type III situation, a region of positive valence and a region of negative valence are in the same psychological direction from the person: they are functionally similar or perhaps identical. Psychological movement toward or away from regions is determined by the relative strength of the pertinent forces at the time of movement.

Superficially, Type I and Type II situations appear much alike; however, they are crucially different. A person in a Type II situation is like a ball being pushed from opposite directions by two sticks; once it gives a little, it flies off to the side, out of the picture. A person in such a situation is trying to escape two opposite negative driving forces and is likely to become completely frustrated and, like the ball, leave the field—psychologically either to flee from the scene or become irrationally aggressive. In simpler terms, this means that a frustrated person engages in either actual or imaginative *flight* or *fight.* In contrast, a person in a Type I situation, like a ball being pulled in opposite directions, usually will stay in the field, i.e., remain engaged with the problem and try to resolve his conflict at the level of reality at which he meets it. He is influenced by, and attracted toward, two psychologically opposite goals, both of which have positive valences. The goal toward which he moves is the one with the higher value or valence. (Should his two opposing goals be exactly equal, would he be like the donkey who starved to death while standing exactly halfway between two stacks of hay?)

Since Type II conflict situations—those containing two opposite negative goals—give rise to frustrations, they should be avoided in teaching procedures. Contrastedly, since Type I situations—those containing two opposite positive goals—involve and perplex but do not frustrate students, they should be sought.

An example of how a Type III conflict situation develops is a person's contemplating violating one of the basic mores of his society, especially if it is for the first time. He wants to perform the tabooed act and simultaneously he wants not to do it. Thus, it has both positive and negative valence. If the positive valence is the greater of the two, he performs the act. In another, similar situation, the person involved might perceive the taboo, not as a negative-goal region but as a barrier between his person and the positive-goal region. In this event, if the act is to be performed, the negative valence of the barrier would need to be counteracted by the stronger positive valence of the act.

What level of tension is best?

A characteristic of the kind of goal-centered situations that we have described is the presence of a certain amount of felt tension or discomfort. A person confronted with a no-path or forked-path situation feels to some degree doubtful, puzzled, bewildered, and uncertain. How strongly he feels this way depends upon at least four factors: (1) the nature of the goals and the person's relationship to them; (2) the desirability of the goal or goals; (3) the apparent difficulty of the intervening obstacle; and (4) his own personality makeup. Depending upon circumstances, the desire to move toward each goal in a problematic situation may range from a mild and easily cast off tickle to a powerful urge capable of commanding all of one's resources. Whether a person finds himself between opposite positive goals that he is trying to achieve or opposite negative aversions that he is trying to escape depends largely upon *how he construes himself and his psychological environment.*

In a sense a teacher must be a tightrope walker. He will get the best results if he keeps his students in a state of full enthusiasm. When he has involved them to the point where they sit on the edges of their seats during discussions, with arms waving, eyes glistening, and all wanting to talk at once, he has a potentially fine teaching situation. When he achieves this, he may be sure that intrinsic motivation at its best is operating. However, there is a rather fine line between this type of situation and one in which students become so excited that their emotions are chaotic. Then, too, they may feel despair because the problem posed is too difficult or become bored because it is too easy. In any of these instances, a worthwhile teaching-learning situation can evaporate suddenly, either through the situation's getting out of hand or students' becoming apathetic.

Necessity for a teacher's maintaining control of the teaching-learning situation cannot be overemphasized. One of the difficulties that commonly arise when a teacher attempts reflective teaching is loss of control. Any class engaged in problem-centered study will seem rather disorderly, but teachers often err in mistaking unproductive chaos for relaxed but healthy work-related involvement.

HOW DOES PROBLEM RAISING PROCEED?

We have been considering when a problem is a problem, how a problem is a felt tension, and the level of psychological tension that is best. We now proceed to a study of the basic procedures that are involved in reflective teaching and learning. These include both problem-raising and problem-solving techniques. Problem raising is a process of persons' discovering and identifying inadequacies and disharmonies in their outlooks or the cognitive structures of their life spaces. Problem solving, in turn, is a process of reconstructing outlooks or cognitive structures so as to make them more adequate and harmonious. Problem raising is the first of the five aspects of reflective thinking; problem solving encompasses the other four (see pages 166–172). Problem raising consists of both recognition and definition of a problem.

A problem arises in the thinking of a student whenever, by some means, he is induced to be either dissatisfied with, or doubtful concerning, some aspect of his present knowledge, attitudes, or values. The dissatisfaction or doubt represents a forked-path, blocked-path, or no-path condition within the student's life space that is characterized by conflicting goal regions. When a student has a real problem, he should be asking himself: "Is an existing insight, attitude, or value adequate, is it valid, or is an alternative to it more promising? In adherence to a given pattern of thought, is there a basic contradiction? What are the real issues in regard to the ideas that I hold? What are the available alternatives in thought and action?"

Whenever two or more competing alternative ideas, attitudes, or values are at stake, there is an *issue*. Since, by definition, all issues are controversial, *controversy is a fundamental aspect of any truly problem-centered teaching*. Controversy involves either interpersonal or extrapersonal conflict. *Interpersonal conflict* arises when respective individuals or groups hold ideas that are sharply opposed to those of other individuals or groups. We often refer to conflicts of this type as "controversial issues." Persons on each side of an interpersonal conflict or dispute may be quite consistent, each in his own outlook, even though the outlook is in sharp disagreement with that of the opposing party. In our culture such conflict may arise between social classes, between racial, religious, ethnic, or age groups, between capital and labor, and between the sexes.

When a student becomes aware of his own incompatibilities of outlook, the resulting internal struggle may be referred to as an *intrapersonal conflict*. The content of an intrapersonal conflict may be no different from that of an interpersonal one. Yet it tends to foment greater tension in the individual. Since *extreme* intrapersonal tension is hazardous to an individual's personality structure, this level should not be deliberately promoted. Nevertheless, for a reflective learning situation to exist at all, issues must come to be felt by students in such a way that each finds himself to some degree in controversy with himself. Hence, each individual must be attracted to some extent by two or more competing hypotheses and feel temporarily unable to make a choice between them; otherwise, for him, no problem exists. Accordingly, if teachers are to teach reflectively, they must help students expose contradictions and inadequacies in their thinking and action to their own critical examination.

How may teachers bring students to recognize contradictions and inadequacies in their thinking?
For a teacher to accomplish much in helping students see their inconsistencies, he needs a good idea of what kind of contradictions his students are likely to hold. This knowledge will enable a reasonably skillful teacher to pursue a line of discourse and questioning that will expose a student's ideological inconsistencies and inadequacies to himself. Some techniques for exposing contradictions and inadequacies and thereby raising problems in the thinking of students are the teacher's use of a *subject matter switch,* his introduction of *disturbing data,* his permitting students to *make mistakes,* and his helping students *convert some societal problems into personal ones.* The examples of these techniques that we give are hypothetical ones and, of course, are very much simplified. To make the contradictions and inadequacies explicit to most students in a class, much more discussion than is herein described would be necessary.

A *subject matter switch.* A subject matter switch is accomplished when a teacher helps a class generalize—reduce to a principle—a particular idea that is expressed by a student, then demonstrates how a further thought that is held by the same student is incompatible with the generalized principle and, consequently, with the first idea. For example, a student expresses the opinion that "Government price supports for cotton are ridiculous." The teacher then seeks agreement with the principle that "the federal government should not interfere with the economy." The teacher then places the principle in a different context, that is, gives it a different subject matter with a question like "Do you favor a protective tariff on cotton?" The student, who also adheres firmly to the principle that "a high protective tariff brings prosperity to a nation," is placed in a position that forces him to make some kind of revision of either one or both of his contradictory opinions, should he attempt to extricate himself from the contradiction. To achieve the desired result, the teacher must hold the student closely to the issue. If a student is permitted to qualify his opinions by introducing exceptions, he may extricate himself readily without having to do any serious thinking.

Teachers should realize that often, when a subject matter switch does not provoke thinking in the particular student who is trapped by it, it does motivate constructive thought in several other members of the class. The word *trapped* is used here advisedly; yet some rationale for its use is needed. A teacher who wishes to teach reflectively is probably justified in using almost any device that helps get reflection going. Some such devices may seem so teacher-centered that the whole procedure may appear to be rigged in favor of the teacher's biases. But, this is only the beginning aspect of an inquiry. When it comes to casting and scrutinizing hypotheses and drawing conclusions there should be no rigging. Although the teacher performs key functions throughout the reflective process, the relationship between the students and the teacher is centered in mutual inquiry.

Introduction of disturbing data. Another means of inducing students to feel problems is to introduce them to data from outside their life spaces which have the effect of making them doubt some currently held item of knowledge, attitude, or value. The teacher may ask students to read a book, to watch a television program or motion picture, to go on a field trip, or to engage in some other activity that confronts them with facts contrary to those they have taken for granted. Of course, this approach, like any other, may not work. Students may refuse to admit the new facts into their life spaces. Unless they recognize the significance of the facts and truly come to doubt their existing ideas, no problem is created.

Permitting students to make mistakes. Teachers usually do not let students make enough mistakes. Making a mistake often encourages a student to reexamine something he had previously regarded as true. Positive relativists think that it is much more educative to let students do something their own way, experience the consequences, and see their mistakes than to tell them the "right way," which they then follow more or less blindly. Of course, some situations preclude this. A shop teacher might achieve maximum student motivation for study of safety practices by allowing a student to cut off a finger with a power saw, but he would not be morally justified in using such means to establish an efficient learning situation. However, a teacher has many opportunities to permit students to make "problem-raising" mistakes without endangering anyone.

The essence of a problematic situation is that there is something in it that is unknown. The unknown can be uncovered only through some right questions being asked. Some of the best questions are also the simplest: "Why?" "Why did you say that?" "Why do you have the opinion that you have stated?" Because of the demise of several fish in the classroom aquarium, a class of fourth-graders embarked upon an enthusiastic study of the biology and ecology of fish life. The students had been caring for the fish according to what they thought were "right principles." These included the assumption that fish need to eat as much in proportion to their size as do fourth-graders. The teacher, whether or not by design, allowed the children to make a mistake—to overfeed the fish. He then posed the question, "Why did the fish die?" and thereby launched a reflective study.

Converting societal problems into personal problems. There are numerous areas of adult and societal concern about which students normally have some more or less superficial attitudes, evaluations, and knowledge. These include politics and government, international affairs, economics, business, labor and employment, pure and applied science, religion and morality, various arts, and personal relations. The ideas that students have acquired are often sketchy, disorganized, and poorly understood. Nevertheless children, and especially adolescents, do have attitudes, beliefs, and some knowledge about most operations with which adults are concerned. This can be demonstrated by a reasonably free classroom discussion of any one of these subjects. Our question now is, How may a reflective approach to learning serve to build a psychological bridge between adult-societal problems and student-personal concerns?

When students appear in public school classrooms, the total knowledge, both true and untrue, that they have is usually more than teachers realize. With modern media of communication, frequent opportunities for travel, and continuously rising educational levels of parents, it seems likely that a great many youngsters have more factual knowledge than they can make much sense of. So one of the major jobs of a modern school is to help students both verify and make sense of the welter of information that they acquire outside their schools.

Although students willingly make statements about matters in such areas as government, economics, international affairs, and the relationship of science and religion, the commitment that they feel toward such statements varies greatly. In some instances, a student's commitment is so slight that he will abandon a pet idea with little hesitation. At the other extreme, statements may represent convictions so highly cherished and strongly held that a student resists bringing them under any kind of critical scrutiny.

Ideas and attitudes that students hold concerning matters that are also of concern to adults constitute the psychological bridges between youth and adult interests. If a student feels enough personal attachment to a view to care, the moment the position becomes a subject of doubt he is likely to want to start thinking about it. At that point, if teaching is skillful, he can be led to want to study a subject about which he previously felt little or no curiosity. For example, if a considerable number of students in a class think that "most businessmen are dishonest," and the teacher can create sufficient doubt of this notion, students may want to make a study of general business practices. They may want to know what motivates businessmen, and what the consequences of such motivation are. There is no telling where critical analysis of such a problem might lead. Hopefully, it would spearhead inquiries into the most important aspects of our economy.

The point is that by using students' present attitudes, goals, and knowledge as a lure, teachers can often arouse genuine interest in situations that otherwise would never have been felt by students to be in any way problematic. Consequently, in relation to areas in which students at first feel no personal goal or involvement, a learning problem can be created and thereby genuine student involvement can be achieved. Accordingly, students can be led to see that their problems involve the various subject matters of the social sciences, the natural sciences, and the humanities.

A *teaching-learning unit on race: its problem-raising aspect*

The problem herein described was selected through the author's conversations with a number of high school students. The students had various definitions of the term *race*, they recognized that their definitions were cloudy, and they wanted to bring them into sharper focus. So, it was assumed that for most high school students of today the meaning of *race* probably constitutes a real problem. It also was assumed that this problem could emerge in a senior problems, social studies, history, psychology, sociology, or biology class on any one of the four high-school grade levels.

The problem and the aspects of its solution were developed by means of members of an undergraduate class in educational psychology playing the roles of high school students. Throughout the unit the teacher is designated by "T" and each of the participating students by "S." All members of the class participated to some degree, but respective students are not identified. Only the more incisive and significant statements are recorded; limited space precludes our including every detail of the class discussion. To repeat, problem raising consists of both *recognition* and *definition* of a problem. The class discussion proceeded as follows:

T: I noticed in our reading assignment for today that the term *race* appears several times. What does that word mean to most of you?

S: Why, there are three races—white, black, and yellow.

S: I don't think it is that easy, I know some white people who are called Negroes.

S: To me, *race* is a cultural word, the color of people's skin is not the real difference.

T: When you say there are three major races, are you stating the way things really are or are you merely classifying people for convenience? In other words, what is the basis for your distinction?

S: Biologists say that there are three races, maybe four.

S: That may be so, but cultural differences are also called racial features. For instance, people in the United States think of Jews as a race and in Germany Hitler talked about the Nordic race.

T: When people refer to the Jewish race, are they thinking of biological traits, social traits, or what?

S: They are thinking about the fact that Jews have been different down through history.

T: Oh! then we identify them as a race because of their ancestors?

S: Partly because of their ancestors, but also because of things they do, such as make money.

S: We are getting clear away from our discussion; one's race depends upon his genes.

T: So, you think race is purely biological. How many of you think race is purely biological? (A show of hands indicated that about one-half of the class would answer this question in the affirmative, but the other half definitely would not.)

T: So, according to biologists, there are three definite races plus a fourth that even the experts can't agree upon. Then this fourth could be almost any group, so the problem of race is wide open.

S: It is not quite that way. We can limit our definition of *race* to inherited physical characteristics that one group, and not others, has. It is the physical characteristics of a person and his ancestors.

T: For instance?

S: Color of skin and type of hair.

S: But, as I see it, everyone to some degree has a mixed blood.

T: Do you mean that everyone is some sort of a hybrid?

S: I think we're making too much of this. Race is simply a biological variation of *homo sapiens*—a subdivision of the species.

S: Then, according to you, it is very easy to place each of us in a certain race.

S: I'm beginning to think that we should just quit talking about races; we should do away with the idea.

S: We can't do that. *Race* means something to everybody; if they didn't have the word *race*, they would use some other word.

S: The trouble is that race started as a biological word, then people have added a lot of other meanings to it.

T: Let us be more specific in regard to our problem and the issues involved. Just what are we trying to decide?

S: What a race is.

T: O.K. How many of you want to pursue this question further and attempt to arrive at an answer? (Most of the class members favored this procedure.)

T: All right, now we may look at a word in at least two different ways. Do specific Races, each spelled with a capital R, exist in the very nature of things, the way gravity and the planets supposedly do, or is a race merely what people call it?

S: I'm not sure I understand the first meaning, but I am more concerned with the second.

T: You may recall that a few weeks ago we developed the difference between realism and nominalism in regard to the source of large concepts. The question that I am raising is, Do we want to find the *real* meaning of a concept Race, which transcends or extends beyond any and all existing races, or do we want to conceive of race as a name for an idea that men have developed?

S: I, too, am more concerned with the second type of meaning.

T: How many prefer to concentrate upon the meaning of the named idea *race* and leave any transcendental or absolutistic definition out of our discussion? (Most students agreed with the two who had expressed more interest in the nominalistic meaning.)

T: O.K. We shall assume that a word means what it means because of the meanings people give it, not because of its being derived from some basic transcendental source. Now, we must decide one more question. Are we concerned with what the word *race does* mean, what it *should* mean, or both?

S: When we discussed democratic and reflective procedures, we decided that we should study both how things are and how they should be.

T: Any other reaction or ideas?

S: How much are just *we* going to change things by thinking how *race* should be defined?

S: I get your point. But how much are we going to change things by merely studying how things are? I think we should figure out both what *race* means and what it should mean.

T: How many concur with this position? (About two-thirds concurred; the other third expressed the idea that their treatment would be too superficial to attempt any "oughts" in regard to the meaning of the word.)

The next step was to make a precise statement of the problem at hand through using the contributions of the students. The statement of the problem was then reworded until it was acceptable to all members of the class. The problem was: "What does the term *race* mean to all kinds of people, including experts, and what should it mean to us?"

At this point, we should remind ourselves of the fact that in any fertile group inquiry, two types of discussion are always in progress—one the public discussion that an observer can hear, the other a series of private discussions within which each interested student debates the issue with himself. Most of the questions and assertions that are uttered aloud emerge from, or are influenced by, the concurrent private, silent debates. The primary aim of vocal discussion is to help each individual in the classroom, including the teacher, push forward his private thinking. Hence, during the course of a single discussion, Mary may reach a conclusion that seems quite satisfactory to her, John may have his faith in a conclusion that he once held badly shaken, and Fred may merely formulate a hypothesis. In each case, the student may have thought the problem through to a further degree than at any previous time. Hence, in a discussion that appears rather chaotic to an observer, members of the group involved may actually achieve a considerable amount of pointed thinking.

HOW DOES PROBLEM SOLVING PROCEED?

Problem-centered teaching does not end with the inducement of psychological tension. Helping students see problems is just a beginning; it is only the first of five aspects of reflective teaching-learning. However, this aspect is very important in that it provides the motivation and direction for the problem-solving aspects of reflective inquiry. Once doubt or uncertainty has been induced, reflective teaching and learning enter the problem-solving phase.

Problem solving consists of formulating and testing hypotheses; it envelops the last four aspects of the reflective teaching-learning process. Formulation and testing of hypotheses should be conducted in an atmosphere which resembles as far as possible that of a scientific laboratory. The same open-minded and objective attitudes that characterize any scientific investigation should prevail. Hence, the teacher's role should be analogous to that of a head scientist in a laboratory; he should help students construct hypotheses, then assist them in testing them out.

Formulation of hypotheses and deduction of their logical implications

Formulation of hypotheses—considered guesses or hunches—constitutes the second aspect of reflective learning. Deducing the logical implications of the hypotheses constitutes the third. Often, the two aspects are so intermingled that it is difficult to distinguish one from the other. In reflective teaching, students are encouraged to formulate as many hypotheses as possible in regard to what might resolve the discrepancies or inadequacies in thought that have been exposed. Simultaneously, a class is urged to deduce as many of the logical implications of each hypothesis as its members can muster. Within this aspect students think, "If this hypothesis holds, what checkable consequences should result from its operation?"

In the unit on the meaning of *race,* hypotheses are the various alternative definitions of the concept. We now proceed with the second and third aspects of the unit (the first aspect is delineated on pages 163–166.)

T: Let us restate our problem. It is, "What does race mean to all kinds of people, including experts, and what should it mean to us?" Now, let's see how many possible answers there are to this question.

S: The use of the word race does a lot of harm, and no good; let's drop it.

S: But, there are some racial characteristics.

T: For example?

S: Sickle cell anemia is characteristic of Negroes.

T: Is this a disease?

S: Yes, and its incidence is much higher in Negroes.

T: Could you say that a person who has sickle cell anemia is a Negro?

S: No, I couldn't do that.

T: If a person has three white grandparents and one black one, which race is he a member of? (This question opened up a great deal of discussion and disagreement.)

T: Can we say that, even though a person is much more "white" than "black," in the U.S.A. he is a "black?"

S: Are we concerned with the definition of the word in this country?

S: This should be our first concern.

S: If we even do this, we will be doing quite a lot.

S: Some minority groups think they can help their position by emphasizing their race.

S: But other racial groups have made themselves a part of the American culture. Chinatown has been pretty American.

S: A member of any minority group has things stacked against him.

T: This morning on the "Today Show" a Negro professor at a New York university appeared. New York public universities pay top salaries. Do you think this man still finds the cards stacked against him?

S: Yes, I do.

T: How many agree that he does? (About one-half of the class agreed.)

T: It now seems to be the time for us to "handicap" ourselves with some information. Let's all go to the library and find at least one article on the subject of race. Each of you be prepared to give us the high points of what you find out.

At the next class, students in turn contributed the ideas that they had gained through their reading. The teacher then asked each student to write out, in one short paragraph, the very best statement on, or definition of, race that he could devise.

Between classes the teacher and several class members summarized the contents of the statements. The summary in terms of the ideas stated and their frequency was as follows (ideas stated only once are not included):

1. Race primarily is a biological concept. (15 times)
2. In light of the improbability of there ever having been any pure races, the increasing miscegenation—cross-breeding—that is occurring, and the emotionality surrounding the term *race*, the concept of race has always been ambiguous and is now becoming archaic. (13 times)
3. The term should be either discarded or disregarded. (11 times)
4. The only term with which people should be concerned is the *human race*. (4 times)
5. A biological definition is inadequate. (3 times)
6. We can't ignore the term, so we should understand it. (3 times)
7. *Race* should be replaced with *ethnic groups*. (2 times)

This summary was dittoed and distributed in the next class. The various ideas were taken as hypotheses whose implications were to be tested through further reading and thought.

Testing hypotheses, the fourth step

In the fourth aspect of reflective thinking, teaching, and learning, *students are encouraged to examine the hypotheses in the light of all obtainable, pertinent evidence.* Provided the teacher promotes an atmosphere of mutual inquiry, problem-centered study in school may encompass a variety of evidence-seeking activities. It is likely to include the use of individual and group research, home study, field trips, and guest speakers. It may also include considerable explanation and illustration on the part of the teacher. An informal lecture can be a highly useful tool both for providing data for students' consideration and for instigating and promoting further reflection.

In the process of testing hypotheses, a teacher does not play the role of a softhearted baby-sitter. At times he must be quite tough-minded in his insistence that students examine and consider all pertinent available evidence. He also must guard against students' making hasty generalizations, arriving at snap conclusions, achieving premature closure, or taking other liberties that either impede or pervert the reflective process.

Testing hypotheses concerning the meaning of race

At this point in the study of the meaning of *race* the class reviewed the summary of hypothetical statements. The instructor next divided the areas and sources of inquiry among the students so that the investigation would be reasonably comprehensive. The entire class moved to the library during several class meetings to gather as much more pertinent information as possible in the time available. Then, the students returned to their classroom and continued their inquiry.

First, several students presented definitions that they had taken from dictionaries, encyclopedias, and other books. Next, other students presented some new ideas that they had gained from their reading. At this stage of the study several sharp disagreements arose. Samples of student expressions are as follows:

S: Why are we talking about race at all? We are just building up more prejudice and racism.

S: Each individual has his own definition, so let's let it go at that.

S: Cultural distinctions are not racial ones.

S: William A. Boyd and Isaac Reisman, in *Races and People,* say that physical features are useless criteria of race.

S: Although a biological definition is the most ideal, it is not the most practical. A word can mean many things to people.

S: The best we can do with the word is to try to understand what it really means in relation to the evolution of man, to separate fact from fiction, and to pass on our knowledge to others. Then, hopefully, as people learn to live together, the word will disappear from their vocabularies.

S: Ashley Montagu, in *The Concept of Race*, says that the term *race* has had a long and tortuous history. Biologists see it as the subdivision of a species, and laymen have an emotionally muddled interpretation of the word. But anthropologists see the term as facts forced into predetermined categories. The major idea he brings out is that the meaning of the term *race* is far from being a solved problem, and that man generally refuses to see this. The ethnic groups formed by virtue of community, language, religion, and social beliefs just add to the confusion. If *race* is to be a scientific term, it must have a genetic meaning; geographical, linguistic, and ethnic grouping then would be unnecessary. However, race is a trigger word because it is loaded with prejudice and misunderstanding.

S: If we are to form an operative definition of race, we should limit it to the inherited physical characteristics that are predominant in one group of people as opposed to another group. The prejudice implied in the word *race* should be limited to the words "prejudice" or "bias" so as not to confuse Jewish "race" and Negro race and consider both to be races.

S: Basically, there are physical differences in people. Therefore, people need some way of explaining or understanding this. The word race is an attempt to do this. It describes three (or possibly more) sets of physical characteristics, each set belonging to one of the races. It should be based only on these biological aspects, because within each race there are many cultures.

S: Race started out as a biological term, but society has taken the term and added other meanings to it. The easiest answer would be to do away with the word, but I think that it is here to stay for a long time yet, and if we're going to find answers to our problems today the change is going to have to come from within the people themselves. The older generations won't or can't change their feelings and ways of thinking, so it is up to the younger generations to accept changes in their society, and this takes time.

S: I think that defining *race* biologically is a complete waste of time and meaningless. *Race* does, however, imply or refer to characteristics that *exist* in some way or another, and quite obviously it causes much strife within our society. So, I think that we can't ignore the term.

Arriving at conclusions, the fifth aspect

The fifth aspect of reflective teaching-learning is *drawing consions*. This is perhaps the most difficult aspect of a teacher's endeavor to promote reflective learning through reflective teaching. However, the basic, guiding principle of reflective teaching and learning is that the teacher and students should strive to achieve at least a consensus on the conclusion, unanimity being the ideal. But even though a student may represent a minority of only one person, he should not be coerced in any way to swing his position to the conclusion of either the group consensus or the majority.

So, ideally, problem-centered study should culminate in at least a tentative conclusion about how the problem might be alleviated or solved. However, in many instances a definite conclusion will not be achieved. Furthermore, when a conclusion is reached, the teacher should emphasize its tentativeness and relativity. An irrevocable conclusion is like a locked door whose only key has been thrown in the sea. Students should be taught that the door to knowledge must always be left unlocked, or even ajar. Nevertheless, at the termination of an inquiry, a conclusion should be considered to be a warranted assertion; it should provide greater predictive accuracy than any alternative hypotheses that have been entertained and examined.

A conclusion may involve either reacceptance of the idea that was originally brought under question, modification of the idea, or formulation of a substitute one. The important concern is that students push their thinking further than it had gone before. Reaffirmation of the same idea that the teacher had earlier induced students to doubt is quite acceptable, provided that in the course of their study the students come to understand the idea better and to have a better grasp of the evidence pertinent to it.

Conclusions of the study in regard to the meaning of race

The high school class had completed the first four aspects of reflective inquiry. It had stated the problem in definite terms; it had formulated some hypotheses and deduced their implications; and it had gathered much pertinent data and tested the various hypotheses. The culminating task was to formulate a tentative concluding statement in regard to the hypothesis or hypotheses that seemed most tenable.

In drawing the class's conclusions, the first step was for a committee to construct a carefully formulated summary which incorporated the statements earlier listed as hypotheses. The class then discussed each clause of the summary, and either made changes in it until a consensus would support it, or deleted it. The teacher reminded the students that their decision should rest upon what the data—pertinent information—supported, not personal whims. Out of a class of thirty, there were from none to three dissenting votes in regard to the final form of each clause. The class's concluding statement in regard to the meaning of the term *race* was as follows:

Since we cannot ignore the concept *race* in our American culture, we need an understanding of its meaning. Race is primarily a biological concept. But a biological definition, in itself, is inadequate; cultural aspects also enter into its meaning. Because (1) there is an improbability of there ever having been any pure races, because (2) miscegenation is increasing, because (3) the concept *race* serves little long-range beneficial personal-social purpose, because (4) it has been and continues to be ambiguous, and because (5) it is emotionally loaded, the term *race* now should either be discarded or considered archaic. So, we should move toward elimination of the concept *race* as such. The only race with which enlightened people should be concerned is the *human race.*

T: Does our conclusion imply that we should strive to build one unified culture to replace various racial cultures? If so, should the one culture be a pluralistic one; that is, should it be one that reflects a unity of peoples, but recognizes and accepts diversity within the unity? Or, should people attempt to blend themselves into one generalized race? Perhaps these questions involve problems for our further study.

The teacher then urged dissenting students to develop cooperatively an alternative statement that they would support and report it to the class. These students were allotted some class time to do this as a group. The teacher also reminded the class of the many insights or understandings that they had gained during their study. These ranged from simply learning some new words—for example, *miscegenation*—to gaining a more meaningful and effective grasp of the race problem. The class then moved ahead to a new problem or area of inquiry.

Throughout the study, the teacher had to make it clear that he preferred and expected serious thinking on the part of his students. His role had been to elicit compelling questions pertinent to the area of study and to lead the ensuing inquiry along lines of gathering pertinent evidence and doing logical thinking.

REFERENCES TO SOME PROGRAMS AND EPISODES OF REFLECTIVE TEACHING AND LEARNING

Bateman, Grant, William Lieurance, Agnes Manney, and Curtis Osburn, *Helping Children Think.* Tri-University Project in Elementary Education. New York: New York University Press, 1968.

Pages 6–8, 19–21, 26–31, and 49–79 describe approaches to,

and units in, teaching reflectively in the various elementary grades. Pages 81–97 contain "springboard" questions that may be used to initiate reflective learning. This book is probably the best source for elementary school teachers.

Bayles, Ernest E., *Pragmatism in Education.* New York: Harper & Row, Publishers, 1966.

Pages 109–127 depict elementary school units for teaching spelling, arithmetic, art, nature study, and grammar reflectively. Pages 127–140 describe secondary units in literature, American history, and natural science.

Bigge, Morris L., and Maurice P. Hunt *Psychological Foundations of Education,* 2d ed., New York: Harper & Row, Publishers, 1968.

Pages 337–338 give examples of insightful learning. Pages 405–407 describe teaching at the ninth-grade level through reflective means. Pages 573–575 report an actual unit that was used in teaching a high school English class reflectively. Pages 545–547 describe reflective teaching of the meaning of the concept *mind* on a college level.

Brunner, Jerome S., *et al., Studies in Cognitive Growth.* New York: John Wiley & Sons, Inc., 1966.

Chapters 3 through 12 present research studies of cognitive growth of children. The studies are concerned with intellectual growth as it is affected by the way people gradually learn to represent their worlds through action, imagery, and symbolizations. Thus, the chapters describe children's solutions of problems and thereby provide patterns, but not specific details, for reflective teaching.

Engelmann, Siegfried, *Preventing Failure in the Primary Grades,* Chicago: Science Research Associates, 1969.

Chapter 4, "Reading for the Nonreader," explains how to teach reading in order to help children *get the ideas* surrounding the use of words. Hence, it opens the way for a teacher to teach beginners how to read, using reflective processes.

Gage, N. L., ed., *Handbook of Research on Teaching.* Chicago: Rand McNally & Co., 1963. Chapter 17, "Research on Teaching the Social Studies," by Laurence E. Metcalf.

Pages 941–943 present two reflective units, one on who discovered America by Bayles and one on the election of 1800 by Griffin.

Hunt, Maurice P., and Laurence E. Metcalf, *Teaching High School Social Studies,* 2d ed., New York: Harper & Row, Publishers, 1968.

Pages 1–18 depict a reflective study of two revolutions, the American and the French. Pages 71–72 outline a history lesson taught reflectively. Chapter 10, pages 207–236, provides examples of the five aspects of reflective teaching.

Jones, Richard M., *Fantasy and Feeling in Education.* New York: New York University Press, 1968.

Pages 28–33 present a fifth-grade lesson on Eskimo culture taught on an understanding level. Pages 33–46 describe teaching fifth-graders about Eskimo infanticide on basically a reflection level.

Wertheimer, Max, *Productive Thinking,* enlarged edition edited by Michael Wertheimer. New York: Harper & Row, Publishers, 1959.

The entire book provides ideas and designs for reflective teaching in mathematics and physics.

SELECTED REFERENCES*

Adler, Mortimer J., and Milton Mayer, *The Revolution in Education,* Chicago: The University of Chicago Press, 1958. (rational realism)

Ayer, A. J., *The Problem of Knowledge,* Baltimore: Penguin Books, 1956. (logical empiricism)

*The philosophical positions that appear in parentheses after some of the entries indicate which of the basic, systematic, educational philosophies the respective entry harmonizes most closely with, and contributes to.

Barzun, Jacques, *The House of Intellect*, New York: Harper & Row, Publishers, 1959. (rational realism)

Bateman, Grant (Associate Professor, Bemidji State College, Bemidji, Minn.), Lieurance, William (Associate Professor, University of Wyoming, Laramie, Wyo.), Manney, Agnes (Professor, University of Cincinnati, Cincinnati, Ohio), Osburn, Curtis (Associate Professor, Indiana State University, Terre Haute, Ind.), *Helping Children Think: Report of the Implementation of a Teaching Strategy*. This study was conducted within the Tri-University Project in Elementary Education at New York University, 1967–1968. Sponsored by the Office of Education, United States Department of Health, Education and Welfare.

Bayles, Ernest E., *Democratic Educational Theory*, New York: Harper & Row, Publishers, 1960. (positive relativism)

Bayles, Ernest E., *Pragmatism in Education*, New York: Harper & Row, Publishers, 1966. (positive relativism)

Bayles, Ernest E., and Bruce L. Hood, *Growth of American Educational Thought and Practice*, New York: Harper & Row, Publishers, 1966.

Bigge, Morris L., *Learning Theories for Teachers*, New York: Harper & Row, Publishers, 1964.

Bode, Boyd H., *How We Learn*, Boston: D. C. Heath & Company, 1940. (positive relativism)

Bronowski, J., *Science and Human Values*, New York: Harper Torchbooks, 1956. (positive relativism)

Broudy, Harry S., *Building a Philosophy of Education*, 2nd ed., Englewood Cliffs, N.J.: Prentice-Hall, Inc., 1961. (rational realism)

Brubacher, John S., *Modern Philosophies of Education*, 3d ed., New York: McGraw-Hill Book Co., 1962.

Brumbaugh, Robert S. and Nathaniel M. Lawrence, *Philosophers on Education*, Boston: Houghton Mifflin Company, 1963. (Chapters 2, 3, and 5—rational realism; Chapter 6—positive relativism)

Butler, J. Donald, *Idealism in Education*, New York: Harper & Row, Publishers, 1966. (idealism)

Butler, J. Donald, *Four Philosophies and their Practice in Education and Religion*, 3d ed., New York: Harper & Row, Publishers, 1968. (Part 3—idealism; Part 4—rational realism; Part 5—positive relativism)

Cantril, Hadley, ed., *The Morning Notes of Adelbert Ames Jr.*, including a correspondence with John Dewey, New Brunswick, N.J.: Rutgers University Press, 1960. (positive relativism)

Childs, John L., *Education and American Pragmatism*, New York: Holt, Rinehart and Winston, Inc., 1956. (positive relativism)

Conant, James B., *Modern Science and Modern Man*, New York: Doubleday & Company, Inc., 1953. (positive relativism)

Dewey, John, *Reconstruction in Philosophy*, New York: Mentor Books, 1950, originally published by Henry Holt, 1920. (positive relativism)

Dewey, John, *Human Nature and Conduct*, New York: Holt, Rinehart and Winston, Inc., 1922. (positive relativism)

Dewey, John, *Art as Experience*, New York: Capricorn Books, 1958; originally published by G. P. Putnam's Sons, 1934. (positive relativism)

Dewey, John, *Experience and Education*, New York: The Macmillan Company, 1938. (positive relativism)

Dewey, John, *Theory of Valuation*, Chicago: The University of Chicago Press, 1939. (positive relativism)

Dupuis, Adrian M., and Robert B. Nordberg, *Philosophy and Education*, Milwaukee, Wis.: Bruce Publishing Company, 1964 (Chapters 1–5—rational realism)

Frank, Philipp, *Relativity—A Richer Truth*, Boston: Beacon Press, 1950. (positive relativism)

Geiger, George Raymond, *John Dewey in Perspective*, New York: Oxford University Press, 1958. (positive relativism)

Gibson, James J., "The Concept of the Stimulus in Psychology," *American Psychologist*, vol. 15, 1960, pp. 694–703.

Henry, Nelson B., ed., *Modern Philosophies and Education*, Chicago: The University of Chicago Press, 1955. (Chapters 2 and 3—rational realism; Chapter 4—idealism; Chapter 5—positive relativism; Chapter 9—logical empiricism)

Hullfish, H. Gordon, and Philip G. Smith, *Reflective Thinking: The Method of Education*, New York: Dodd, Mead & Company, 1961. (positive relativism)

Hunt, Maurice P., and Lawrence E. Metcalf, *Teaching High School Social Studies*, 2nd ed., New York: Harper & Row, Publishers, 1968. (positive relativism)

Hutchins, Robert M., *The Learning Society*, New York: Frederick A. Praeger, Inc., 1968. (rational realism)

Kneller, George F., *Introduction to the Philosophy of Education*, New York: John Wiley & Sons, Inc., 1964.

Krutch, Joseph Wood, *The Measure of Man*, Indianapolis, Ind.: Bobbs-Merrill Company, Inc., 1953. (rational realism)

Krutch, Joseph Wood, *Human Nature and the Human Condition*, New York: Random House, Inc., 1959. (rational realism)

Kuhn, Thomas S., *The Structure of Scientific Revolutions*, *International Encyclopedia of Unified Science*, vol. 11, no. 2, Chicago: The University of Chicago Press, 1962.

Leonard, George B., *Education and Ecstasy*, New York: Delacorte Press, 1968. (existentialism)

Martin, Wm. Oliver, *Realism in Education*, New York: Harper & Row, Publishers, 1969. (rational realism)

May, Rollo, *Psychology and the Human Dilemma*, New York: Van Nostrand Reinhold Company, 1967. (positive relativism)

Meyer, Agnes E., *Education for a New Morality*, New York: The Macmillan Company, 1957. (positive relativism)

Morris, Van Cleve, *Existentialism in Education*, New York: Harper & Row, Publishers, 1966. (existentialism)

Morris, Van Cleve, *Philosophy and the American School*, Boston: Houghton Mifflin Company, 1961.

Murphy, Arthur E., *The Theory of Practical Reason*, LaSalle, Ill.: Open Court Publishing Co., 1964. (positive relativism)

Neff, Frederick C., *Philosophy and American Education*, New York: Center for Applied Research in Education, 1966. (Chapter 2—idealism; Chapter 3—rational realism; Chapter 4—positive relativism)

Reid, Louis Arnaud, *Philosophy and Education*, New York: Random House, Inc., 1962.

Shermis, S. Samuel, *Philosophic Foundations of Education*, New York: American Book Company, 1967.

Skinner, B. F., *Contingencies of Reinforcement: A Theoretical Analysis*, New York: Appleton-Century-Crofts, 1969. (logical empiricism)

Skinner, B. F., *Walden Two*, New York: The Macmillan Company, 1948. (logical empiricism)

Skinner, B. F., *Science and Human Behavior*, New York: The Macmillan Company, 1953. (logical empiricism)

Smith, Philip G., *Philosophy of Education*, New York: Harper & Row, Publishers, 1965. (positive relativism)

Thayer, V. T. and Martin Levit, *The Role of the School in American Society*, New York: Dodd, Mead & Company, 1966.

Walker, Marshall, *The Nature of Scientific Thought*, Englewood Cliffs, N.J.: Prentice-Hall, Inc., 1963.

Wann, T. W., ed., *Behaviorism and Phenomenology*, Chicago: The University of Chicago Press, 1964.

Wiener, Philip P., *Evolution and the Founders of Pragmatism*, New York: Harper Torchbooks, 1965; originally published by Harvard University Press, 1949. (positive relativism)

INDEX

70 71 72 73 7 6 5 4 3 2 1